WITHDRAWN

L. R. COLLEGE LIBRARY

363.1966
H91m

110628

DATE DUE			

MIRROR IMAGE

MIRROR IMAGE

Nancy Hunt

MIRROR IMAGE

CARL A. RUDISILL LIBRARY
LENOIR RHYNE COLLEGE

HOLT, RINEHART AND WINSTON · NEW YORK

363.1966
H91m
110628
July 1979

Copyright © 1978 by Nancy Hunt
All rights reserved, including the right to reproduce
this book or portions thereof in any form.
Published simultaneously in Canada by Holt, Rinehart
and Winston of Canada, Limited.

Library of Congress Cataloging in Publication Data
Hunt, Nancy.
Mirror image.
Autobiographical.
1. Change of sex—United States—Biography.
2. Hunt, Nancy. I. Title.
RC560.C4H85   363.1'9'66 [B]   78-4690
ISBN 0-03-040646-3

First Edition
Designer: Amy Hill
Printed in the United States of America

Permission to quote excerpts from the following
publication is gratefully acknowledged: *Transsexualism
and Sex Reassignment*, edited by Richard Green, M.D.,
and John Money, Ph.D. (Baltimore: The Johns Hopkins
University Press, 1969). Copyright © 1969 The
Johns Hopkins University Press.

To Ellen

WHO LOST HER LIFE
WHILE SAVING MINE

MIRROR IMAGE

ONE

The University of Virginia Medical Center sprawls on the side of a hill, an array of red-brick Georgian buildings, some dating from the last century, placed at different angles and elevations and connected by arcades, tunnels, and walks. Even the staff members have trouble finding their way through this maze. Visitors inevitably get lost.

The best way to get from one part of this complex to another is probably to go outdoors and start over. On better acquaintance, one discovers the institution's major corridors, the yellow-tiled arteries that lie along the buildings' ventral surfaces with frequent capillaries departing left and right to such organs as X-ray, private urology, outpatient surgery, and physical therapy. Through these vessels flows the medical center's human bloodstream: nursing students in blue uniforms, medical students in beards, residents carrying clipboards, Pink Ladies with gray-blue hair fastidiously fingerwaved, janitors, pharmaceutical salesmen, ashen-faced surgical patients, senior attending physicians, mutilated children, apprehensive wives, lab technicians,

1

X-ray technicians, dieticians, auditors—all pulsing through the corridors until late into the night.

At the end of one of these corridors lie the operating rooms, accessible through a pair of sliding doors that open at the touch of a panel mounted on the wall. It's a hard place to find and a forbidding place to enter unless you have business there. Trespassers are challenged by nurses posted like sentries in a glass-walled station just inside the sliding doors. "Can I help you?" one of them asks in menacing tones.

Next to that glass sentry box, a plastic notice board, as high as the ceiling and as long as an automobile, bears the day's surgical schedule with the pertinent facts about each patient spelled out in black grease pencil.

The second name on that schedule one recent summer day was that of Elizabeth Johnson. I stood before the notice board and read the data that had been written in the ruled squares beside her name: She would be in Operating Room No. 11, her surgeon would be Dr. Futrell, the procedure would be a vaginal construction. The box labeled PRE-OP DIAGNOSIS had not been filled in.

I already knew J. William Futrell. He had been my own surgeon six months before in one of these operating rooms for a procedure similar to the one Miss Johnson was about to undergo. But many others would crowd into Operating Room No. 11 that morning, including sterile and circulating nurses, anesthesiologists, an intern, and a senior resident. There would be a medical illustrator perched on a metal stool, making quick pencil sketches for possible use in medical journals and textbooks. And because of the interest in this bizarre operation, there would be a covey of students and doctors who had contrived their excuses and their schedules to watch the work. (At one point during the procedure, I was to count sixteen people around the operating table, jockeying for position, craning backs and necks, striving for a peek.)

By the time I entered, attired in a green operating-room gown, a paper beret over my hair, a paper surgical mask over the lower half of my face, and a pair of electrically conductive paper bootees over my shoes, Miss Johnson had already been anesthetized. A tube ran into her mouth and down her trachea to keep her airway clear, held in place by a strip of plastic tape that bit deeply into her lower lip. This intubation bared her teeth in a fixed and inappropriate half-smile. Two more strips of tape ran diagonally across her eyes to keep the lids closed. As part of her preoperative medications, she had been injected with scopolamine, which, among other things, would make the patient dry-mouthed and would allow the corneas to become dry if the eyes remained open.

Only a few wisps of hair escaped from Miss Johnson's paper hat. The profound sleep induced by the halothane anesthetic had left her inert. Except for the rhythmic rise and fall of her rib cage, she looked like a corpse, even down to the *risus sardonicus*, the smile of death.

In another setting, she was a pretty woman of thirty-five with rust-red hair and a quick, gentle laugh. I had met her the previous night in her hospital room, which coincidentally adjoined the room that I had occupied for twenty-nine days. Her supper lay cold and untouched on the bed table. She was too nervous to eat it, she said, and anyway, what was the point when before the evening was out she would be subjected to laxatives and enemas until she was physically and emotionally empty? I thought she was right.

And so we talked about ourselves and our medical problems and the hazards of succeeding as women in a man's world. She was English by birth, employed as an engineer in a company that built nuclear power plants. I was a newspaper writer and editor. We both had endured the resentment of our male colleagues, coupled ambivalently with their amorous advances. In this she had probably suffered more than I because she was prettier and given to coquettish mannerisms. She had a habit of tossing her head almost imperceptibly so that her soft, shoulder-length hair swung attractively, at the same time casting her eyes aside in a way that seemed to make them sparkle. I assumed that she had practiced this before a mirror, and she readily confessed that she liked to "look pretty."

She had achieved that ambition. Like most women, she had flaws—a nose too sharp, hands and feet too large, forearms too long—but her figure, for all I could see of it as she lay on her bed in a gray hospital gown, was good. (She told me with some pride that she had a twenty-five-inch waist.) In preparation for her hospitalization, she had had a good haircut with a slight flip at the ends. Her smile was quick and warm, and her face was animated, with large, dark eyes of remarkable beauty.

I couldn't see her eyes now in the operating room. The diagonal strips of tape gave her the grotesquely bleary look of a drunk in a comic strip. Three I.V. bottles were dripping their contents through plastic tubes and needles that pierced the back of her left hand. One of the anesthesiologists was trying to run another needle into a vein in her neck. I could not—did not want to—imagine that all of this had been done to me scarcely six months before.

I could only dimly recall the journey to the operating

4

room, my mind already fuzzy from pre-op medications, my mouth dry, the lights of the yellow-tiled corridors floating overhead. Then a pause in a tiny, yellow-tiled chamber, the induction room. Somebody was swabbing the back of my left hand with disinfectant. "Now you're going to feel a little bee-sting," a voice said soothingly, as if talking to a child. I felt the sting—then mercifully nothing more until I awoke in my room six hours later. Had I really lain there where Elizabeth Johnson lay now, transfixed, defenseless, exposed?

Washed in the glare of the enormous overhead lights, her body looked emaciated and chalky. Her breasts were small and high, like those of a twelve-year-old girl. At one end of the table, two anesthesiologists bent over the grinning mouth and the x'd-out eyes. At the other, her feet hung suspended in stirrups, forcing her knees up and back and apart in the lithotomy position. Her pubic hair had been shaved. And there, forced upward into the cruel light, were Elizabeth Johnson's fully developed male genitalia—the anomaly, the detested excrescence she had borne all her life. In the next few hours, that growth would be excised.

Jeffrey L. Marsh, the chief resident in plastic surgery, stepped forward between the widespread legs, slid his hands beneath the small of the back, and lifted the patient a few inches toward him. His eyeglasses glittered above his mask. Marsh is a thin, incisive man in his early thirties, a scholar and a technician and—when he can manage it—a demon Alpine skier. As a surgeon he is very good indeed. And like most doctors in teaching hospitals, he is also a teacher, a role that he took a moment now to fulfill.

"What's the difference between a heterosexual, a homosexual, a transsexual, and a transvestite?" he asked, addressing the short, plump intern who had just begun her rotation in Plastic Surgery.

"I haven't had a chance to read up on that," she answered uncomfortably.

Marsh was placing drapes, like green bedsheets, over the patient's abdomen and legs, leaving only the perineum—the crotch—exposed. "A heterosexual," he said as he worked, "is someone whose genital sex coincides with his psychological sex and whose love object is of the opposite sex. A homosexual is someone whose genitalia, psychological makeup, and love object are all of the same sex.

"A transsexual," he continued, "is someone whose genital sex and love object are the opposite of his psychological sex." Elizabeth Johnson was a transsexual. So was I.

"And a transvestite is just someone who gets a personal thrill out of dressing up in the clothes of the opposite sex."

During this impromptu lecture, Futrell had entered the operating room. As senior surgeon, it was his prerogative to arrive after the patient had been prepped by his subordinates. Futrell is only a few years older than Marsh and in fact looks younger, with a boyish face and the build of a college football player, which indeed he once was. Transsexual patients often become infatuated with their surgeons, and Futrell must have had his share of this kind of adoration.

Futrell took his position at the patient's left hip and leaned over the abdomen so that he could work on the operating field from above. Marsh, standing between the legs, would work from below. At times, the tops of their heads would almost touch. As they discussed the work in progress beneath their hands, their voices would remain so low as to be almost inaudible to others in the room.

"Can we have a sopping-wet sponge, please, and then a dry one?" Marsh asked.

The sterile nurse, standing on a stool behind the patient's left leg, with instruments arrayed on tables both in front of her and to one side, prepared the sopping-wet sponge and handed it to Marsh. She had a slim, young body and lovely eyes that looked out gravely from above her mask. She had covered her hair with a flower-print scarf instead of a commonplace paper hat like mine. What does this solemn, pretty girl think, I wondered, as she gazes upon this anatomically male patient who has come here to be unmanned? Does she feel contempt? pity? revulsion?

I already knew what Futrell thought, having asked him the previous day. We had talked in his tiny, cluttered office, which, along with the ritual diplomas and photographs of medical colleagues, was decorated with pictures of his children and of Futrell himself in action on the football field.

"You're so obviously delighted to be a man yourself," I said, "and so devoted to your wife and children, what do you feel emotionally when you obliterate this organ that symbolizes virility?"

"I don't feel anything," he said. "To me it's just a surgical procedure." He paused and chuckled. "But we have a standard joke in the operating room when we're doing one of these cases. When we cut off the first testicle, there's always somebody who goes 'Ugh!'"

Surgeons tend to take a pragmatic view of these matters. Patients will want a face lift or a rhinoplasty (nose bob) or breast augmentation, and the plastic surgeon obliges on the grounds that, while the medical necessity may be trifling or altogether absent, the emotional need may be desperate. The removal of the penis fits neatly into this philosophy. But the same does not always hold true for other medical specialists. Urologists, for example, often have reservations, as one of them told me a few days after my conversation with Futrell.

"The plastic surgeon is very accustomed to the fact that the patient is displeased with himself and wants to do something about it," said Dr. Edwin D. Vaughan, a University of Virginia urologist who had participated in my own operation. "But for the urologist, it's different. Our whole existence is directed toward preserving these organs. We reconstruct penises, bring down undescended testes, and repair hypospadias, so we're sort of geared to making that set of organs functional. The concept that someone wants to give them up is foreign to us."

Foreign, perhaps, but not unknown. Vaughan was still an intern when he saw his first male transsexual who had amputated his own penis. He has seen many others since.

Yet the transsexual population, while never precisely measured, constitutes only a minute fraction of the male sex. Most men, like most women, treasure their genitalia. Sometimes in Vaughan's practice he has to tell a patient that he must be castrated in order to fight prostatic cancer. Frequently, the patient weeps.

But no one wept for Elizabeth Johnson that morning, and least of all would she have wept for herself had she been awake. When I talked to her the preceding evening, she had been as elated as a bride about to meet her bridegroom. I had felt the same way the night before my own surgery.

Marsh drew the path of the incision, marking with heavy black lines on the patient's white, shaven skin. On the scrotum he drew diagonal, crosshatch lines. Then he took a small knife, and at 10:32 A.M. he began to cut.

"Sponge," he said as the blood welled.

"Sponge."

"Clamp."

"Clamp."

As they worked, Futrell would hold a piece of tissue out of the way while Marsh cut, and a moment later Marsh would hold while Futrell cut. They discussed each step, their voices low, relaxed, as if they were calculating chess strategy. Today's operation would differ in several particulars from the one I had undergone, and undoubtedly their future sex-reassignment surgery would differ yet again. Most surgeons use the same procedure for years, but the University of Virginia people don't believe that they have evolved the single, perfect method, and so with each patient they try to improve their technique. In the relatively short history of sex conversion, there has been plenty of room for improvement.

Surgeons have been trying to construct vaginas at least since 1817, when Baron Guillaume Dupuytren is said to have undertaken the task for a woman who had been born without one—a predicament known as vaginal agenesis. Similarly, for the next century and a half, all subsequent attempts at vaginal construction were performed on women, it being seldom supposed that a man would have any desire for such an organ. For raw materials they tried to make the lining out of almost any tissue they could think of: the skin, a portion of hernial sac, amniotic membrane, or peritoneum. In 1904 a surgeon named J. F. Baldwin even tried using a suitable length of intestine, but this didn't work because the neovagina kept oozing digestive juices in continuation of the tissue's original function.

The skin graft method commonly employed today was devised in 1937 by McIndoe and Counseller. In this procedure, the surgeons take a split layer of skin, usually from the inside of the thigh or the buttocks, where the scar will not be noticeable.

To create a vagina for a woman was socially acceptable.

To do the same thing for a man was not, although there is record as early as 1931 of a crude sex-reassignment operation performed by F. Z. Abraham, a German doctor, on a transsexual Danish artist. The patient did not long survive the surgery. For the next twenty-one years, little or nothing was done in the field. But in 1952 an ex-GI received surgery —simple castration with no vaginal construction—in Denmark from a team headed by Dr. Christian Hamburger, then returned to the United States as Christine Jorgensen, indisputably the most widely known transsexual of all time. In some ways Miss Jorgensen's example retarded as well as advanced the cause of sex reassignment. Denmark promptly amended its laws to make it impossible for another foreigner to follow in her steps and the blaze of publicity attendant upon her triumphant return to the States (EX-GI BECOMES BLONDE BEAUTY) horrified the U.S. medical profession. Although the public was absorbed by Miss Jorgensen's act, appalled doctors felt that if they did in America what Hamburger had done in Denmark, they might find themselves shunned by their colleagues, even in danger of losing their hospital and university affiliations. To this day, the field of transsexual surgery has been illuminated by only a few acts of courage on the part of the U.S. medical profession.

"Certainly physicians are a very conservative bunch, politically and every other way," Vaughan told me. "Sexually they are very sheltered. They are goal-oriented. They go for that medical degree from the time they're in high school, and they have little time for social life or dating. What's more, there are virtually no courses on human sexuality in medical schools. So with their natural conservatism and their lack of experience, this is a real problem for physicians."

One of the first American physicians to attack the problem was Milton T. Edgerton, now chairman of the department of plastic surgery at the University of Virginia. A man of great professional eminence today, he has often risked his reputation and his career by using surgery to relieve emotional suffering. While on the staff of the Johns Hopkins Hospital in Baltimore, he was one of the first surgeons in the United States to perform augmentation mammaplasty, surgical enlargement of the breasts. Outraged, his professional peers conspired to discredit him at a convention where he was to present a paper on this work, but so persuasive were his arguments that the designated accuser underwent a change of heart and led the applause instead.

In the surgical treatment of transsexuals, Edgerton has met still stronger condemnation.

"I started the first clinic in this country which offered surgery to transsexuals," Edgerton told me recently. "That was at Hopkins in 1963. I had been seeing transsexuals who had been operated on in Mexico, California, Casablanca, Denmark—anywhere they could get the operation done. And it was awful work. By taking care of these people who had been botched, I got to know them and became aware of their problems. They were nice people, and I observed a curious thing about them: They were always grateful to their doctors, even those who had botched the job. They seemed to feel that 'At least he was willing to help.'"

From repairing the work of others, it was a logical though perilous step for Edgerton to initiate his own work.

"The atmosphere was just dynamite for six or eight years," he told me. "A lot of my colleagues thought I was crazy. The climate has changed now, but ten years ago it was a real no-no to be involved in this work. It was so bad that my wife would be embarrassed when people found out her husband was involved. It takes a bit of a thick shell to go ahead in the face of that kind of opposition."

If the opposition was great, the unmet need was even greater.

"All nonsurgical methods of treatment undertaken to help these patients have been uniformly unsuccessful to date," Edgerton told a meeting of the American Association of Plastic Surgeons in 1969. "Without treatment, many transsexuals become socially maladjusted, gravitate toward lives of crime, and spend countless hours and considerable money in pursuit of medical help; many terminate these unhappy and maladjusted experiences with suicide. Respectable medicine has rarely bothered to take a second look at these tragic people."

Edgerton doesn't claim that the solution to the transsexual's dilemma resides solely in the scalpel. "I would never want to be quoted as saying that surgery is the answer," he told me. "I hope it's not. But psychotherapy, electric shock, and drug therapy have all failed. In fact, there's essentially a zero cure rate for all nonsurgical methods of treating transsexuals that have been tried."

As a transsexual, I could understand the reason for this failure. I didn't want to be "cured," to be reconciled to my male anatomy. I wanted to be rid of those hated organs, to be granted a body in harmony with my nature. If some hypothetical doctor had approached me with a syringe and promised that one injection would cure me forever of my compulsion to be a woman, I would have fled in terror. No woman would abandon her psychological gender merely to accommodate herself to the circumstances of a biological accident. Certainly I would not. Let the biological accident be corrected, not me.

As it happened, Edgerton and Futrell together corrected my accident with a little help from Vaughan, who hooked up my urethra. In other cases the surgeons dispense entirely with the urologist and do the plumbing themselves. Conversely, a gynecologist may sometimes assist in the operation, depending on the procedure used.

"We use new modifications in almost every case," Edgerton told me. "Usually these modifications promote better healing, but not always. Our goal is to be safe, to use the minimum number of operations, and to achieve a result that is as functional as possible. In the case of the newly constructed vagina, that means it will have a natural appearance and be capable of feeling sensation in intercourse."

In this, few surgeons equal Edgerton and his colleagues. While the Edgerton team painstakingly constructs labia and clitoris, others sometimes leave nothing but a crude slash. The Edgerton technique constructs the vagina out of penile tissue, a tricky procedure because of inherent problems with blood supply. Most others use split-skin grafts, which are inferior in both elasticity and sensitivity. Furthermore, skin grafts taken from almost anywhere except the penis of a genetic male are likely to produce hair. The earliest sex-change operation pioneered at Hopkins used the scrotum to construct the vagina, but even in its new position, the scrotal tissue continued to grow hair, forcing the alumnae of this procedure to douche repeatedly with a depilatory.

At 10:47, precisely fifteen minutes after the first incision was made, Futrell was slitting open the length of Elizabeth Johnson's penis, from the glans to the base, snipping with a pair of scissors. Later, when the skin of the penis was turned inside out and placed inside the patient, the glans—the tip end—would form the vault or roof of the vagina and in this position would bear a remarkable resemblance to the cervix of the normal female uterus.

Marsh was tying off a large blood vessel. Smaller vessels were merely cauterized, and for this purpose another surgeon stood by armed with an electric cautery. Upon a signal from Marsh or Futrell, he would lean forward and apply the two tines of the cautery, and a tiny wisp of smoke would rise from the severed end of the vessel. One time the cautery accidentally touched Futrell's hand, and an electric current found its way through a microscopic and unsuspected hole in his surgical glove. Futrell jumped as if he had been burned, which he had, and stepped away from the table to get a new glove. A few minutes later, the same thing happened to Marsh. Neither surgeon complained or raised his voice.

"How's it going?" Edgerton asked amiably. Unnoticed by either Futrell or Marsh, the chief had entered the operating room, capped and masked but not gowned, having come merely as an onlooker and adviser. They were trying a new, one-stage procedure—which ultimately failed—and Edgerton wanted to keep an eye on things, especially the circulation to the neovagina. The others deferentially made room for him at the table, but I was surprised to detect no disruption in the prevailing calm. Edgerton, I had been told by friends who had watched my own surgery, was a tartar in the operating room, quick-tempered and critical.

I confess I had never found him so myself. With me he had always been gentle and understanding. In his first letter, months before I met him face to face, he wrote, "Your sense of humor remains undaunted, and that is an admirable quality." He had found the exact words to win my devotion.

Now Edgerton observed the work in progress, then wheeled up a Hasselblad camera, mounted on boom and dolly, and took a series of photographs, both for the patient's record and for possible publication in medical journals, for which he writes numerous articles, not necessarily on sex conversions. His fame, in fact, rests more solidly on

14

his work in craniofacial surgery, the reconstruction of children's malformed heads and faces. This is formidable surgery, often requiring the relocation of eyes, noses, and even brains. At the other end of the scale, Edgerton had devoted the previous afternoon to reshaping the arms of a woman who thought them too fat.

After he had taken his pictures and asked a few tactful questions, Edgerton withdrew, and Futrell and Marsh got on with their work.

"This one is coming out nicer than any we've done," Marsh said in a pleased voice.

"Can we check on that blood?" an anesthesiologist asked the circulating nurse. They like to have plenty of donor blood crossmatched and ready for use, although the patients seldom need it. The surgery is carried out under hypotensive anesthesia, which slows the bleeding but requires meticulous monitoring of the patient.

The visiting surgeons were crowding forward, acutely interested.

"You leave the corpora intact, do you Bill?" asked one.

"Uh-huh," Futrell answered.

They were proceeding today on the assumption that an intact corpora would aid circulation. In other neovaginal constructions, this tissue is discarded.

"Can I have a sitting stool, please?" Marsh asked.

The circulating nurse pushed a wheeled stool against the backs of Marsh's legs, and he sat down to work. He had been operating for more than an hour. Merely to stand there watching for that length of time had begun to tire me.

Marsh was now excavating the vaginal pocket, the space between the rectum and the bladder that would be occupied by the vagina, just as in a genetic woman. It's a tricky bit of dissection at first, cutting a path through the central tendon of the perineum and the central fibers of the levator ani muscles. Once past that barrier, however, it's a simple job of "blunt dissection," just pushing things aside with gloved fingertips.

"She's got a narrow pelvis—really narrow," Marsh commented as he worked his fingers in more deeply. Surgeons always take care to refer to male transsexual patients with feminine pronouns. "It's terribly important as a doctor to feel the gender of the patient," Edgerton had told me. From our first meeting months before, he had felt me to be a woman despite my male anatomy. He wouldn't have operated on me otherwise.

"Do you see the prostate?" Marsh asked the intern at his left elbow. "Now it's small because she's been on estrogens." Virtually all male transsexuals have been taking these female hormones for months or even years before surgery, with consequent breast development, muscle loss, and redistribution of body hair and fat. The male beard, however, must be removed by electrolysis, a process that in my case required treatment one hour a week, at twenty dollars an hour (forty dollars at the shop where I started) for three years—and the rates have increased since then. Nor do the estrogens raise voice pitch; to acquire an acceptable female vocal range takes practice and discipline. In female-to-male transsexuals, androgens, or male hormones, usually stimulate beard growth and lower the voice. (The only female transsexual I ever knowingly met wore lumberjack boots and had a big bushy beard, a fine deep voice, and a build like a wrestler.)

By 11:52, an hour and twenty minutes after the first incision, Marsh was fitting the newly made vagina into the vaginal pocket he had just prepared. "That's sitting back in there well," he observed. For the first time in her troubled life, Elizabeth Johnson had genitalia to match her mind. I felt it was a sublime moment, and I wished she were conscious so I could tell her and share her happiness.

"How much blood do you figure she's lost?" Futrell asked.

"Oh, I'd say two or three hundred cc's," an anesthesiologist answered. "Tell you exactly in a minute."

An insignificant amount.

The major part of the operation was now complete. Mostly all that remained was the suturing, the painstaking sewing with each stitch placed to minimize bunching and scarring. At one point, disliking what he had just done, Marsh snipped and removed an entire row of sutures and started over again from the other end.

Lunchtime had come and gone, and so had many of the onlookers. Futrell had retired to an adjacent utility room and was clowning for a friend of mine, a student nurse who was giggling uncontrollably.

At 2:10, Marsh was sewing in the urethral meatus, the opening through which the patient would empty her bladder. In the male, the urethra—the tube that conveys urine from the bladder to the meatus at the tip of the glans—is about eight inches long. In the female, since it doesn't have to run the entire length of the penis, it's very much shorter, usually about one and a half inches. This shorter distance is less inhibiting to microbes, making women far more susceptible to bladder infections than men. Miss Johnson's urethra had been greatly reduced in length, and from now on, like any other woman, she would have to look out for bladder infections.

Except for the rows of sutures, like railroad crossties, on

either side of her labia and running in a single line up the lower part of her abdomen, Miss Johnson now looked like the normal, anatomical woman she had always aspired to be. Just below the pubic bones and at the top of the line of sutures in the perineum, Marsh had left a small flap of tissue. He now began to abrade this with tiny scalpel cuts.

"Is that your clitoris?" asked one of the few remaining visitors.

"Going to be," Marsh answered. He fastened it in place with a few quick sutures.

And presently the job was done, at 2:45 P.M., just four hours and thirteen minutes after the first incision and approximately six hours after Miss Johnson had been wheeled out of her hospital room, leaving her male past behind her. The nurses looked pale and tired. I myself was hungry and exhausted. Miss Johnson, still unconscious but with the strips of tape removed from her eyes, looked as if she had been carved from white wax. Futrell was still joking in the utility room. Marsh, his shoes and gown stained with blood, looked like the survivor of an Indian massacre.

But when I met him a few minutes later in the hospital snack bar over cheeseburgers and coffee, Marsh was quite indistinguishable from the auditors and pharmaceutical salesmen at the other tables. His scholar's face gave away nothing of fatigue or triumph. He discussed the operation in quiet, precise language, then dumped his paper plate and napkin in the trash can and disappeared down the corridor. For all I know, he spent the afternoon performing another operation.

TWO

Early that evening I called on Miss Johnson in her hospital room. She had recovered some of her color, her hair had been combed, and she was lying beneath her sheet with half-closed eyes. There was a quality of serene beauty about her face, something that reminded me of the sort of painting that used to be entitled *Rest after the Storm.*

Yet the storm had left its mark on her. She really looked dreadful. An I.V. tube was running into her arm—its drip rate a trifle slow, I thought critically—supplying her with fluids, nourishment, and medications. She would not be allowed to eat for a couple of days, and even then she would get only Jell-O, tepid clear soup, and coffee. A catheter snaked discreetly from under the sheet, draining her bladder into a plastic bag tied to the side of the bed. Both her I.V. and catheter were probably functioning more efficiently than her mind, which would still be addled from the aftereffects of the anesthetic. It was, I knew, the bleakest hour in the surgical experience.

I put on a smile that was intended to be both warm and reassuring. "Hi, Liz, how are you feeling?" A stupid question, asked with numbing repetition in hospitals, but perhaps stupid questions are most easily fielded by addled minds.

She turned her head slowly toward me, as if the effort cost her dearly in energy and pain, and held out her hand. She wore a contented smile. "Hello, Nancy," she said, taking my hand. "My bladder feels as if it were going to burst."

Her English-accented voice emerged as a faint and painful croak, the result, in large part, of the endotracheal tube having been in her throat throughout the operation. I remembered my own ascent from the foggy abyss of halothane and the simultaneous urgent bladder pressure.

I did now for Miss Johnson the little that had been done for me: I found the plastic surgery resident on duty and asked him to make sure the catheter was running properly. It was.

"They did a beautiful job on you, Liz," I said. "You'll be so pleased when you see. It's everything you could have hoped for." I patted her hand gently, then left her to face the night alone. If her experience were to resemble mine, she was going to have a rotten time.

I can see that evening now with the shocking clarity of a nightmare recalled: the brain disabled, the room swirling, an army of medically garbed figures milling about me as I lay on the cart, hands reaching to lift me onto my bed, little grunts of exertion.

"Get his feet!" the head nurse commanded.

"Not *his*, goddammit!" I rasped, surprised at the soreness of my throat. In the six weeks I spent as a patient in the University of Virginia hospital, it was the only time I heard anyone refer to me with a masculine pronoun, but it was the wrong time.

They transferred me to the bed, hung the I.V., connected the catheter and plastic bag to collect urine, checked my vital signs, readjusted the I.V. drip rate, raised the side rails. I thought I would throw up if the room didn't stop pitching and rolling. I gripped the rails to stabilize the world. I thought my bladder would explode.

"Are you sure the catheter is running right?" I asked plaintively.

Futrell was there with several residents. They checked the catheter. "It's running fine," they assured me.

"Oh, if I could only pee!"

Desperately I looked about the crowded room for the one person I totally trusted, totally loved, the wife of my former male self. We had been divorced just a few days before I entered the hospital, not because the law clearly insists upon it, but because Edgerton wished it and because it's usually done that way in transsexual surgery lest the wife sue for being deprived of the comforts of the marital bed. It was one more price to pay for my compulsion. And it was only logical— women, after all, are not married to women. I hoped that Ellen and I would always remain friends, but for her sake I hoped she would find a normal male to share her life.

I hadn't wanted her to accompany me to the hospital, but again, Edgerton preferred me to have someone there "for emotional support." She had been with me through every step of the transsexual experience from self-revelation to surgery, and it gratified my sense of dramatic unity to have her with me now. Unhappily, she had come down with a virulent case of flu just three days earlier and should have been home in bed, not flying to Charlottesville, changing planes on the way, and hanging around hospital waiting rooms.

My eyes found her now, standing by the window, and I reached out to her, as I had so many times before. "Is my catheter running right?" I rasped. Ellen was a registered nurse herself and, at that moment, for me the sole repository of all medical knowledge. She moved within the circle of light, revealing a face that looked shockingly ill. I stared hungrily at that face, searching it for the well-known expression of love and compassion, but it was hard and closed.

A few more minutes and everyone had departed, leaving me alone to face my ordeal. I felt as if I were suffocating beneath a jumble of stainless steel and plastic: the side rails, the I.V. bottle, the tube running into my left arm, the catheter running out of me, the oxygen outlet jutting from the wall, the water pitcher, the call button, the enormous television set leering at me from a rack above the foot of my bed—all swirling about in a drunken haze. I stared at the room from between the bars of the rails like a prisoner in a cell. Nothing in my physical world made sense. Nothing fell into place. Everything was in seething motion.

I closed my eyes and recalled Ellen's face as I had last seen it before she dragged herself wearily to her motel room. No, I had not been mistaken, I realized with despair. There had been no love in that well-loved face, only contempt and something close to hatred.

Months later she told me about that night. She had moved to her own apartment by then, and whenever we dined together, we fought bitterly. "You looked so awful that night," she said, "and when I looked down at you, all I could think of was, Why would any man want to do this to himself?"

THREE

It's impossible to estimate the number of transsexuals in this country, though that doesn't stop people from trying. In 1968, Ira B. Pauly, a prominent psychiatrist and researcher in the field, guessed that there were 2,000 male and 500 female transsexuals in the United States, or a ratio of 1 in 50,000 men and 1 in 200,000 women. I think he was way off base.

The Johns Hopkins Gender Identity Clinic "received almost 2,000 desperate requests in one three-week period after a single newspaper story," Edgerton told a medical convention. That's almost one response for every transsexual in Pauly's 1968 estimate. Edgerton himself has been quoted recently as setting the transsexual population at more than 10,000, but physicians tend to give conservative estimates, and I suspect his is still far too low.

My own estimate is that there are 350,000 male and 80,000 female transsexuals, or something close to the population of Minneapolis, Minnesota. Like any statistician with an ax to grind, I reach these figures through a combination of shaky arithmetic, dubious assumptions, and simple chicanery. The computation works like this: Out of 1,500 members of my graduating class at Yale University, I know of three transsexuals, including myself. (Renee Richards, the tennis player, was in a later class.) That's a ratio of 1 in 500, which I then shamelessly apply to the national population. When critics object that I simply can't take the Yale class of 1950 as a statistical model for the entire United States, I merely shrug my shoulders and look offended.

Most transsexuals don't advertise their affliction. Edgerton knows one prominent federal judge who is a closet transsexual and lives in terror that he will be discovered and removed from the bench in ruin and disgrace. At home with his wife, Edgerton's friend lives entirely as a woman. A tormented soul like this is unlikely to submit his name to any census of the transsexual population. And I can understand his fear—I once knew a state judge who was professionally destroyed after he was found in a hotel room with a sailor.

At the other end of the spectrum are the screaming transsexuals, many of whom aren't true transsexuals at all but gay or effeminate men. I've met several of these at the electrolysis parlor I have patronized the last few years—limp-wristed, lisping youths, typically employed as female impersonators in nightclubs, supplementing their incomes with $100 fees as male prostitutes and living in scruffy furnished apartments with their homosexual boyfriends. For them, sex-reassignment surgery can be disastrous. Their boyfriends don't want to make love to anatomical women—they would rather make love to other males. And so the changeling is apt to find herself thrown out in the street with nothing to her name but a cheap plastic suitcase and a new vagina.

The screaming transsexuals typically have exaggerated standards of femininity. Not content with the limited breast development, or gynecomastia, that results from the use of female hormones, they indulge themselves with supercolossal breast augmentations—size 40C is not uncommon—and seek out fly-by-night operators to inject industrial-grade silicone into their hips and buttocks, a practice that occasionally kills them. They tease their hair into beehives, cake their faces with showgirl makeup, and display their breasts in skintight, glittery tops with necklines plunging to the navel. Thus attired, they mince on six-inch platforms from one gay bar to another, from one homosexual assignation to the next. As women they are parodies.

But beneath their grotesque exteriors, some of these people are true transsexuals who turn to homosexual relationships because those are the only kind available to them. (Transvestic homosexuals use this rationale too.) All varieties of sexual orientation can be found masquerading behind the transsexual self-diagnosis, but no matter what trappings of femininity they have adopted, one test usually distinguishes straights from gays: The real transsexual harbors an abiding distaste for his own male genitalia, even to the extent of trying to cut them off himself if he can't persuade a surgeon to do it; the homosexual wouldn't want to lose his penis for anything in the world.

When at the age of forty-seven I finally faced the probability that I was myself a transsexual, I made a pilgrimage to the New York office of Dr. Harry Benjamin, who could fairly be characterized as the grand old man of transsexualism. A crusty, German-born endocrinologist, he has been studying the phenomenon since the early 1920s and has fought doggedly for the transsexual's right to medical treatment. No outcast group has ever had an abler champion.

Yet even Benjamin holds no brief for the transsexual personality, of which he has written that "all kinds of objectionable traits may exist. Unreliability, deceitfulness, ingratitude, together with an annoying but understandable impatience, have probably ruined their chances for help in more than a few instances."

The afternoon I met him, Benjamin was within three days of his ninetieth birthday, full of professional honors and retired from active practice. He didn't approve of me and made no effort to hide the fact.

"You've got to remember," he said in a German accent that long residence in the United States had not eradicated, "that your wife enjoys your penis."

But I didn't care. Like all true transsexuals, I felt branded by my male organs. No matter what my opinion of the benighted youths who flitted in and out of my electrologist's office, I was their sister.

With the exception of Elizabeth Johnson and two or three others, I have never met a transsexual I liked. Admittedly, I have knowingly met no more than a dozen. The transsexual sorority appears to be divided into two camps: those who seek out and enjoy each other's company, and those who, like me, feel uncomfortable with other sexual freaks and try to blend invisibly into straight society. My own observations support Benjamin's, that transsexuals are unreliable and deceitful. Unreasonably, however, I resent it when others apply this blanket condemnation to me, as doctors sometimes do.

After I came home from my surgery, I set about finding a gynecologist, a medical specialist I had never needed before. At length I tracked down a man who had been a member of a gender team at a Chicago hospital and made an appointment for six weeks hence.

When the day arrived, I was ushered into an examining room and told to undress. Presently the doctor entered. He was well over six feet tall, mustached, distinguished-looking, and very brusque. I greeted him with such dignity as I could muster in bra and panties, and, without giving me a chance to explain why I was there, he sat down at a little desk and began to take a patient history.

"How many children have you had?"

"None," I answered, not quite truthfully. I had been the father of three children by my first wife, but I knew that wasn't what he meant.

"Have you ever been pregnant?"

"Never," I assured him.

"At what age did you start to menstruate?"

Now this was fun in a way. Any transsexual likes to be taken for the genuine article, and I was face to face with an expert. But I had sat in his waiting room for an hour and twenty minutes, and he still had a flock of patients out there. Plainly he was pressed for time, and I didn't want to antagonize him.

"Doctor," I said, "I'm a male-to-female transsexual."

He glanced up at me furiously. "How did you get my name?" he demanded.

Not "Wow, I never would have guessed!" or "When did you have your surgery?" or even "It takes all kinds." His response struck me as curiously antagonistic and subjective.

"It wasn't easy," I admitted. "I made about twenty calls to the hospital before somebody ratted on you. They're very protective." His hospital had closed down its gender program out of fear of malpractice suits, and everyone connected with it was covering his tracks like a burglar.

The doctor was not to be placated. "I've treated many transsexuals," he declared menacingly, "and I've found

27

them to be most unsatisfactory patients. They don't keep their appointments and they don't meet their obligations." He meant they don't pay their bills.

I saw that the confrontation couldn't deteriorate any further no matter what I said, and I permitted myself the luxury of anger. "Doctor," I said, dropping my feminine diffidence and sounding really ugly, "I'm a responsible adult. I've worked for the *Chicago Tribune* for fourteen years, and if I don't pay your bills, my medical insurance will."

I kept one more appointment with him, but we never learned to hit it off, and eventually I drifted off to find another gynecologist—a woman this time.

Perhaps the greatest medical hostility exists between transsexuals and psychiatrists. I suspect this arises from the fact that transsexualism is resistant to psychiatric treatment. The psychiatrist knows that he probably can't cure his patient's "delusion," and the patient, in return, doesn't want to be cured. Given a choice, a transsexual would never consult a psychiatrist in the first place except for the fact that a psychiatrist's recommendation is usually required for surgery; few doctors will operate without it.

Knowing that he must have the psychiatrist's permission to attain the salvation of surgery, the patient often resorts to devious means. Most have read the literature of transsexualism and know what symptoms they should present, and these they will recite by rote. Because psychiatrists often want to interview members of the patient's family, transsexuals sometimes rehearse their wives and children in the testimony they must deliver, even to the extent of writing down lines to be committed to memory. I have heard of one woman—herself a male transsexual—who was enlisted to portray a patient's wife in psychiatric interviews.

For his part, the psychiatrist knows that many patients presenting themselves as transsexuals are merely gay or transvestic. And he knows that a high number of unsuitable candidates do in fact manage to con their way through the screening, to their ultimate sorrow. One male transsexual, on the eve of her own surgery, told me that she believed that four out of five who receive the operation come to regret it.

Before my operation, at Edgerton's insistence, I went to see the man who then served as consulting psychiatrist to the University of Virginia's gender team. This was something of a formality because I already had my ticket of admission from a psychologist in New York.

The interview went badly from the start. The man kept playing verbal games and cheating at them. When I denied an allegation, he would pounce on me and say, "Aha, I didn't say that; you did!" But I hadn't. As a newspaper writer, I had been conducting interviews for years, and I had learned to watch what I said. Furthermore, I knew most of the little tricks myself and felt professionally insulted that he should try to pull them on me.

"In all these years," he asked, "did you ever seek psychiatric help to handle this problem?"

"No," I admitted. "All the literature on the subject seems to agree that psychiatry has a zero batting average in curing transsexuals."

"Where did you hear that," he sneered, "in one of your transsexual clubs?"

"I don't belong to any transsexual clubs," I replied stonily.

"Well, it's too late now. You're being admitted to the hospital this afternoon, and tomorrow morning they're going to cut your penis off!"

I was shocked, as I was supposed to be, but not for the reason he had intended. I was shocked by his ignorance of the transsexual mind. I was shocked that he would assault a patient's confidence on the eve of major surgery. And mostly I was shocked by his naked hostility. (I am told that when Edgerton learned of this encounter, as he soon did through a friend of mine, he went through the ceiling. The next time I returned to Charlottesville, the gender team had a new psychiatrist.)

Edgerton himself takes a more charitable view. I have heard him say that he likes his transsexual patients, though when pressed, he will admit that he finds some of them trying. But he does attempt to justify them.

"They are frustrated at not being able to get help or acceptance," he told me one day, "and that either makes them react to the point of aggressiveness or it makes them withdraw into a kind of super privacy. The aggressive ones are evangelical. They want to be noticed, and they overcompensate by wanting to talk about it, to do something about it.

"Now a patient who has been in pain for a long period of time is likely to become neurotic. Lots of transsexuals have become neurotic because of the predicament that society has placed them in. It's such an appalling deformity to the patient, and so often society won't permit him to have it corrected.

"Another curious thing I've noticed is that female transsexuals are generally more subdued than male transsexuals. We don't understand the reasons for this."

I think I do. The male transsexual lives under vastly greater pressure than the female. A woman, if she likes, can wear trousers and a necktie, forswear makeup, crop her hair, and talk tough. A male transsexual has no comparable relief. Let him put on a skirt and lipstick and he will lose his job and his friends, and the police will run him into the station and beat his ears off. No wonder the male transsexual develops personality disorders.

"I'm not sure what to say when people ask me if I 'like' transsexuals," Edgerton mused. "I think I often like them as people in spite of their being transsexual. It's not very important to me if patients are transsexual or heterosexual, really. Either way, they can be disruptive personalities. Some of them are very undisciplined and immature. But the whole range of personality types exists."

Futrell approaches the transsexual personality on a less speculative plane. At the outset, he likes to ask them about their criminal records, and because transsexuals are often cast in roles that lie outside the conventional limits of social behavior, an inordinate number of them have had trouble with the law, usually for minor offenses. Futrell accepts this, but only to a point. "I'm not interested in making happy criminals," he says.

He likes to establish, too, that their gender problem has not incapacitated them. "I'm not willing to spend my time on them unless they're willing to help themselves," he told me.

Beyond these mundane considerations Futrell does not venture. "To me," he said, "looking at transsexuals is like contemplating angels. I don't think anybody can put it together."

The baffling heart of the transsexual mystery lies in their unshakable conviction that, no matter what the evidence of their own genitalia, they belong to the opposite sex. No one knows where this idea originates, though doctors—especially psychiatrists—have devoted an enormous amount of time and study to it. Some investigators believe that the condition arises in males because of an unnaturally close relationship with the mother, combined with a father who is either completely absent or cold and withdrawn. The little boy, they theorize, may seek to placate the terrifying father by adopting the mother's feminine wiles. Certainly many male transsexuals are reared under such conditions, but many are not. The thesis lacks the consistency and uniformity one likes to find in scientific reasoning.

Some researchers suggest that the condition is physiological, stemming from a hormonal accident affecting the hypothalamus while the victim is still in the womb. Other equally reputable scientists say this theory is absolute nonsense.

Dietrich Blumer, M.D., a researcher working at Hopkins, once hypothesized that transsexuals might suffer from brain damage, specifically a temporal lobe disorder, possibly from a blow to the head. But then he took encephalograph readings of fifteen transsexuals and had to conclude that "definite EEG abnormalities are not common occurrences in transsexuals."

Richard Green, M.D., who probably knows more than any man alive about transsexual manifestations in childhood, usually tells only what he has observed, avoiding explanations. But the things he has observed would horrify most parents. He tells of:

> · A seven-year-old boy who "had been praying to God to change him into a girl. He had a strong desire to dress in girls' clothing and was inserting building blocks into his slippers to convert them into high-heeled shoes. . . . He preferred the role of mother in mother-father games, and his favorite toys were dolls." His parents said that he had been acting this way since the age of one and a half.

· A boy who "wore his mother's clothes whenever he had the opportunity. His mannerisms were effeminate. He played only with girls and avoided boys' games." He had started his feminine behavior at the age of six, two years before Green saw him.

· A boy of five who "played only with girls, dressed up frequently in his sister's clothing, and preferred doing housework such as washing dishes and hanging wash to playing outdoors with boys."

· Another boy, age five, who "preferred high-heeled shoes from the time he learned to walk and preferred girls' clothing from age two years. When denied access to girls' clothing, he would fly into a screaming rage. He played only with girls' toys, preferred girls as playmates, and was referred to as a girl by other children when cross-dressed. He stated he wanted to be a girl."

· A five-year-old boy who "insisted he was a girl at age twenty-two months. From the time he could walk he stomped around in his mother's shoes. He dressed up in girls' clothing as often as allowed and put stuffed animals under his outfit in order to appear pregnant."

Having examined every conceivable facet of his subjects and their families, Green concludes that "the specific variables which result in transsexualism remain unknown." But he observes that in most cases the transsexual behavior begins at three years old or younger. And he notes that these harassed children "behave in the way adult male transsexuals say they had behaved when they were young." Interviews with the parents of adult transsexuals often confirm these discordant childhood gender preferences. These children in Green's study will almost certainly grow up to be transsexuals—male transsexuals, of course, since all of them are boys.

And that's a curious indication of the common attitude toward gender: It's quite acceptable, even cute, for a little girl to insist on dressing like a boy, to play with electric trains, to fight to join a Little League baseball team, even to pout and declare furiously that she wishes she were a boy. But let a little boy indulge in comparable cross-gender behavior and his parents will pack him off to the pediatrician or the shrink—more out of fear that he may have homosexual inclinations, perhaps, than because they suspect incipient transsexualism. Girls enjoy far greater freedom in this respect than boys, who are bent and harnessed to a cruel and demanding standard. This social pressure heightens the male transsexual's anguish. Some never try to withstand the pain but begin at the age of three to mince about in their mothers' heels. Others obediently stretch themselves on the rack of their parents' expectations until, tormented beyond endurance, they seek relief from the surgeon. (That's what I did, and I didn't begin to crack until I was forty-four years old.) Other male transsexuals never breathe a word of their affliction but carry it, hidden like an untreated lesion, to the grave.

Female transsexuals, though they appear to be far fewer in number, must certainly suffer too. But I find myself curiously unable to relate to them or to sympathize with their tribulations. In fact, I had never given them a thought until one Indian summer afternoon when I went to see Wardell B. Pomeroy, perhaps the country's most knowledgeable authority on sexual disorders, to obtain the necessary psy-chological recommendation for sex-reassignment surgery. It was our second meeting, but the first at which he had seen me dressed as a woman. We talked for a few minutes, there in his book-lined study in Manhattan's East Sixties where the autumn sun streamed through the windows and the tropical fish swam lazily in great, green aquarium tanks. Presently he came to the point on which I had been so long and painfully impaled.

"You ask if I will write you a recommendation for sur-gery," he said. "I will be happy to."

"You think I'm doing the right thing?" I asked tremu-lously.

"I don't think you have any choice," he said.

I had won! Of all the uncounted thousands of sufferers, I would be one of only a small fraction to attain the deliver-ance of the scalpel. I grieved for the others and felt guilty that I should be saved while they were damned. But I re-joiced in my salvation. I had known similar torn feelings in combat when others had died and I had lived. I felt giddy with relief, drunk with happiness. Sunlight had never looked so beautiful, tropical fish never so serenely enchanting, life never so joyful.

"Tell me," said Pomeroy as I gathered my purse and pre-pared to leave, "what do you think of the women's libera-tion movement?"

Liberation from what? I wondered. From the grace and freedom and beauty and emotional spontaneity of woman-hood?

"I guess I'm not very much in sympathy with it," I an-swered.

Pomeroy laughed. "That's typical of male transsexuals,"

he said. "And I'll tell you something else: Female transsexuals are just the opposite; they're the greatest male chauvinists you ever saw."

For a moment I was stunned—in all the years of my plight, I had not once given a thought to women comparably afflicted. I did so now for the first time.

"I think they must be crazy," I said.

And from that day onward, I have seldom permitted myself an action, a word, even a thought that has not been uniquely feminine.

"By ordinary standards, transsexuals are delusional psychotics," writes Arno Karlen in his encyclopedic book, *Sexuality and Homosexuality*. "But some doctors who have dealt with them say that a number are surprisingly healthy by usual psychiatric standards, apart from their female identification."

Being a transsexual is enough to drive anyone mad, a fact that some authorities have found the charity to concede. One investigator, Dr. Ruth Rae Doorbar, commenting on the results of tests she had administered, observed:

> Among the transsexual subjects, there is a fair amount of paranoid ideation . . . ranging from mild suspiciousness of authority figures to quite frank delusions of persecution. Some of these patients have been arrested and put in jail for female impersonation per se, and others for female impersonation which the police thought was a disguise in the commitment of other crimes, particularly burglary. Since they are frequently and quite frankly breaking the law in their transvestite activities, it becomes almost a necessary defense for sur-

vival to be cautious and even suspicious of the
plainclothes detectives who continually try to identify them.

I was never arrested myself, but I was certainly wary. My
own city, Chicago, has an ordinance prohibiting cross-dressing, and the police enforce it zealously.

But the transsexual's difficulties go far beyond the fear of
detection. As Dr. Henry Guze has observed,

> Prior to surgery the transsexual presents a number
> of personality traits which place him in a severe di-
> lemma. He feels different from other males and
> purportedly more like a female. [Yet this] is diffi-
> cult to verify by comparison with persons of nor-
> mal gender orientation. . . . There's an expres-
> sion of profound loneliness and perhaps desire for
> approval which is not forthcoming. In this sense,
> the patient responds with an aggressive demand to
> be changed. Is he thereby creating a woman he can
> accept or is he showing that he is not a threat and
> thus avoiding violence? The interviews with the
> transsexual male reveal an abhorrence of any type
> of aggression in his early life. He might say: "I'm
> really a woman—don't hurt me. I'll do what you
> want." The converse of this for women who seek
> the change to the masculine role is more marked
> aggressiveness and perhaps the ideation: "I'm
> really a man—don't give me special protection, I'll
> take what I want." In either case, the patient in-
> sists that God has cheated him, and there's a tre-
> mendous undercurrent of resentment toward the

Deity and authority. In scaling the patient's behavior, one finds an intense spitefulness in almost all of the persons studied, both men and women.

Guze isn't alone in challenging the male transsexual's womanly credentials. Dr. John Money, a psychologist and celebrated authority on sexual dysfunction, writing in collaboration with Clay Primrose, has expressed the same skepticism. Commenting on fourteen male transsexuals at Johns Hopkins who had taken the Guilford-Zimmerman Temperament Survey Test, which discriminates between the sexes, they observe that "in every one of the cases tested, the male transsexuals scored lower on masculinity than 90 percent of the normal male standardization population. Seven out of eleven scored more feminine than 60 percent of the normal female standardization population."

They concede that "the results of this test indicate a high degree of verbal adherence to feminine stereotypes on the part of male transsexuals." But then they qualify this by saying, "Adherence to stereotypic female behavior norms is not an indicator of all aspects of the psychosexual state, but may be in part the result of a conscious, superficial imitation of female behavior which transsexuals do remarkably well."

You see? There it is again. You just have to watch them all the time or they'll fool you with their clever imitations.

I once took the Guilford-Zimmerman test. It consists of True-False questions that are thought to separate the girls from the boys. Among them:

· You would like to go hunting with a rifle for wild game.
· You can look at snakes without shuddering.

· You would rather study mathematics and science than literature and music.

· You would rather be a forest ranger than a
dress designer.

· The sight of an unshaven man disgusts you.

· When you become emotional you come to the
point of tears.

I had just completed my second tour of military duty
when I took this test and was being interviewed by a voca-
tional guidance counselor to ascertain what I should do
with the rest of my life. I didn't like the man. He had an insufferable air of superiority and an array of prissy mannerisms that struck me as distastefully effeminate. In contrast here was I, a former buck sergeant, tough, profane,
and determined to succeed as a man.

He told me that my test results showed that I was pre-
dominantly feminine. Then he settled back in his swivel
chair, placed his fingertips delicately together, and eyed me
smugly through heavy, horn-rimmed glasses. "What do you
think of that?" he asked ominously.

I thought for a moment in consternation. "I don't know
what to think of it," I said at last. "If it means that I'm an
incipient homosexual, it scares the hell out of me."

"Aha!" he said, pivoting forward in his chair like a snake
about to devour a mouse. "That's just what it doesn't
mean!"

I still think that a preference for books to baseball is a superficial definition of femininity, and yet the test—un-
abashedly based on sexual stereotypes—has a high degree of
statistical accuracy in telling men from women. Though the
liberationists would object, it appears that a significant ma-

jority of men really do want to go hunting with a rifle for wild game, and a significant majority of women really can't look at snakes without shuddering.

I soon forgot entirely about the Guilford-Zimmerman Temperament Survey and didn't resurrect it from the back of my mind until twenty years later when I was forced to confront the essential nature of my sexuality. Even then, I would not accept Money and Primrose's suggestion that I had falsified my answers to make myself sound like a woman. It strikes me as unreasonable to suppose that any man in his right mind would fake the symptoms of transsexualism. After all, there isn't any money in it, and it doesn't advance one's career or win social approval.

Since science has failed to answer the riddles, I'm tempted to believe that the male transsexual's compulsion to be a woman is a joke played by the gods, one of nature's dirty tricks like a birthmark or a club foot, something beyond rational explanation. Jan Morris, the British transsexual and journalist, called it a conundrum—an unanswerable question. It just happens, filling the victim with the inexplicable conviction that despite all physical evidence to the contrary, he is—or ought to be—female.

And it happens in infancy, long before the sufferer becomes aware of the profound social and sexual differences between the sexes. In all of Green's subjects, the onset was observed between the ages of one and a half and four. Jan Morris recalls that she was three or four when the realization came full-blown upon her one day as she was sitting beneath her mother's piano. For myself, I know that by the age of four I was already aware that I had a girl's mind. No one planted this conviction in my brain—it was there from the beginning.

And it has been there in other males, in other cultures, in

other times, since the creation of the earliest myths. The Greek gods even had a member of the Olympian congress whose appointed job was to sympathize with men who longed to be women. The prophet Tiresias was a postoperative, male-to-female transsexual, the surgery having been performed by the gods as punishment. But Tiresias was a two-time loser because, having decided he liked it better as a woman, the gods turned him back into a man. This occasionally happens to twentieth-century mortals, male transsexuals who decide they don't like being women after all; but the surgical restoration of manhood is supremely difficult—only two cases having been reported in medical literature—and is never entirely satisfactory. The gods did it better.

Many classical writers—Hippocrates, Philo, and Juvenal among them—give accounts of transsexuals, both mythological and factual. The Roman emperor Heliogabalus is said to have married a male slave and offered half his kingdom to any physician who could transform him from emperor into empress.

Instances of cross-gender identification appear throughout the Renaissance. Green cites the case of the Abbé de Choisy, a seventeenth-century Frenchman whose mother raised him as a girl and who later wrote: "I thought myself really and truly a woman. I have tried to find out how such a strange pleasure came to me, and I take it to be in this way. It is an attribute of God to be loved and adored, and man—so far as his weak nature will permit—has the same ambition, and it is beauty which creates love, and beauty is generally woman's portion. . . . I have heard someone near me whisper, 'There is a pretty woman.' I have felt a pleasure so great that it is beyond comparison. Ambition, riches, even love cannot equal it." (As a woman who has occasionally been told she is beautiful, I support the Abbé's testimony. There's absolutely nothing to beat it.)

From the eighteenth century comes the classic case of Chevalier d'Éon, from whom the word *eonism* is derived as a synonym for *transvestism*. Known as "the most glamorous transvestite in history," d'Éon participated in the intrigues of the court of Louis XV and executed diplomatic missions to Russia, all in the guise of a woman. Despite the affidavits of distinguished men who were said to have examined d'Éon's body, both before and after death, there remains considerable doubt about whether he was in fact a transvestite, a transsexual, or an anatomical woman.

Many American Indian tribes harbored men who lived as women, and this is true today among Siberians, Eskimos, and African tribes, also in Madagascar, Tahiti, and Borneo. Sometimes these women-men live as priests, sometimes as wives; sometimes they have been given the suggestion of breasts by ornamentation, sometimes they have had their male genitalia ritually mutilated. Although science has failed to define the cause, every age and every land has produced transsexuals. They are a cosmic fact of life.

And writhe though they may, curse God and fight against their destiny, transsexuals know the trick that has been played on them. I myself knew it long years before I first read the word *transvestite*. So deeply ingrained was my longing to be a woman that I believed it must be shared by every boy but that we were all too ashamed to admit it. Not until late adolescence did I begin to understand that my prep school classmates were perfectly content to be males. Then I knew how truly alone I was and had been from the beginning.

"From the time I was born, I knew something was

wrong," Elizabeth Johnson told me the night before her surgery. For one thing, her playmates had treated her like an alien. "Your peers are the ones who pick you out the fastest," she said.

I knew this was true. It wasn't merely that I had cried more easily or hated fighting or thrown a ball like a girl, though these were all facts. It was a deeper difference. I wasn't like them, and they sensed it, smelled it, and in consequence always kept me at a distance, as if I were a threat to them, as if I had been marked for punishment by the gods.

FOUR

The mark the gods put upon me was the organ that mid-
wives and obstetricians examine at birth before they inven-
tory the less important attributes, such as whether the baby
is spastic or blind.

I suppose my father rejoiced when I was born. He had
badly wanted a son to carry on his name and had been disappointed in three previous tries that had resulted in daughters. I was the product of my mother's last, reluctant efforts
to bestow a male heir upon my father. If the chromosomes
hadn't matched up right that time, she was damned if she
would try again. She had had trouble carrying me—kidney
difficulties, blood in the urine—and I was later made to feel
that I owed her an apology for having been a naughty and
inconsiderate fetus. I have devoted considerable energy over
the years to the expiation of this and other offenses.

In the innocence of the nursery, I paid scant attention to
the biological arrangement between my legs, assuming that
everyone was constructed the same way. I simply under-

stood that my sisters were little girls and I was a little boy, and as such we were required to behave differently. This struck me as unjust, since I felt I had as much right as my sisters to be a girl. It did not occur to me that this discrimination was rooted in the mechanism through which I voided my bladder.

When I was five, we moved into a splendid Colonial house, built in 1775. It stood atop a windswept Connecticut hill, surrounded by maples and elms and one towering pine. Vast stretches of lawn and gardens reached out from the white clapboard walls, and beyond these lay hayfields, cow pastures, an orchard, and, at the far edge of our land, a wooded glen and a brook. My parents had bought the place almost as a lark when they had driven up from New York for a Yale football weekend, consummating the transaction with a ten-dollar down payment to the farmer who owned it. After the removal of the chickens from the dining room, the installation of closets and bathrooms, the digging of a well, and the replacement of the cellar stairs, which had been chopped up for firewood, the decrepit farm blossomed anew as an estate befitting our tenuous claim to aristocracy. We were, to be sure, listed in the Social Register, and luscious apples of money grew from some branches of the family tree. My father's father was a widowed and impecunious naval officer, forced by deafness into early retirement, who had contrived to marry a lady of chilly demeanor and enormous wealth. My mother's father was an old dear with a heart of gold and assets to match, the latter amassed in the manufacture of piano keys. My father, who had pursued an uneven career in book publishing in New York, accepted a post in the Yale University Library soon after buying the run-down farm, and then moved his family out of an opulent Manhattan apartment into the Connecticut country-side.

It was a big move, we being ten in number: my father, a dimly perceived power hovering over our destinies; my mother, who had briefly operated a combination tearoom and bookshop but had otherwise consecrated her life to domestic duties; my three older sisters, who were not noticeably attached to me; myself, perpetually bewildered by events; Cathy, my Irish nurse, whom I loved to the exclusion of everyone else; Bridget, Cathy's sister, who was our cook; Jerry, my oldest sister's fox terrier; and Whisky, my middle sister's Irish terrier.

My mother lives in that Connecticut house to this day, alone now except for the field mice that can sometimes be heard scuttling in the walls. She is very ill, and when we talk on the telephone, she says she would like to see me; but that, as my sisters have often told me, is impossible. I did return to Connecticut once after my operation, and even walked past the house which stood in the shadows of the same maples and elms that guarded it when I was a child. I looked longingly at the flagged front walk, the fine Colonial doorway, the flower beds now somewhat in disarray, and the perfectly proportioned windows, behind one of which my mother was resting—lonely, sick, and old. But I could not go to her, not as a woman. I hurried down the hill and did not look back.

My two oldest sisters had their own bedrooms under the eaves on the third floor, while my youngest sister and I had to share the front bedroom opposite my parents' room on the second floor. My nurse had a little bedroom behind mine, and the cook was tucked away heaven knows where.

My sister and I also shared a bathroom, and it was there

one night when I was five and she seven that she drew my attention to the essential physical difference between us. I must have been an unobservant child never to have noticed this earlier, but I was astonished. At first I assumed that she was playing another trick on me, that she had cleverly concealed a portion of her anatomy. But she finally convinced me that it was no illusion, that she was indeed made differently from me, and furthermore that this difference conferred upon her the lofty status of girl while I was condemned to the inferior rank of boy.

I was furious. The whole game was so arbitrary and unfair. Why should she possess this passport to the privileges of girlhood while I was deprived without reason, without hope of appeal? I brooded on this injustice and tried to remedy it. Each time I was left alone in the bathroom, I experimented with various ways of pulling and tugging at myself and clamping my legs together until I thought I had achieved the same effect as my sister, but as soon as I let go, I popped back into the form in which I had been cast. It was maddening. I kept trying until one night Cathy discovered me in the midst of my endeavors and said that if I ever did it again, she would spank me.

Cathy was a pretty, rosy-cheeked girl, convent-reared to love the Virgin Mary and wash all children thoroughly behind the ears. She dressed me in the morning and heard my prayers at night ("Don't forget to pray for your father"), fed me every meal, took me for walks through the fields and down to the plank bridge that crossed the brook, cleaned my nails and brushed my hair, and bought me presents on her Thursday afternoons off—usually little hammers and tin boxes of nails, for which I was grateful since they came from Cathy, though I would have preferred a doll. I lavished all my affection on her, and she loved me in return. Many years later, when she was married and had a son of her own, she sometimes absentmindedly called him by my name.

I recall seeing little of my parents, though my mother now protests that she was in constant attendance upon me. My father I did not know at all. As heir apparent to the chief librarianship at Yale, he held professorial rank and led an active social life with his faculty colleagues, many of whom would drive out from New Haven on weekends to pick string beans in our vegetable garden, talk about books, and sip mint juleps on the stone-floored porch overlooking the flower beds. My mother served as reluctant handmaiden to these lordly councils. Children were excluded.

My father occupied a position at home only slightly lower than God's. To a small child he looked frightening: six foot three with bristly hair, a spiky mustache, and pince-nez that glittered like lightning. In the evening, after he had returned from the office and I had been prepared for bed, Cathy would escort me to the library on the first floor where he sat like Zeus enthroned, drinking a cocktail in his great leather chair in which I was forbidden to sit. In my pajamas with the trapdoor flap, I approached the throne and kissed him good-night, wanting him to hug me and love me but scared of his menacing strength and prickly mustache.

That constituted my daily association with my father. Today when I read about fathers who fish and play ball with their sons, I find the image incomprehensible. I never played with my father. I played with my youngest sister and my nurse.

Among the events that kept me in a continual state of bewilderment was the removal of Cathy and Bridget. Cathy was packed off to my grandmother's house to serve as waitress and parlor maid, leaving me desolate and without an ally. I was often told with exaggerated patience that I had grown too big for a nurse, but this explanation struck me as insufficient. It had never occurred to me that you discard the people you love because their services are no longer required. To succeed them my parents engaged a Finnish couple named George and Annie, he to do the yard work and take care of the cars and she to do the cooking. George was a mechanic of inspired talents, and I used to follow him worshipfully as he constructed his inventions: a light that lit automatically when a car entered the garage, a buzzer that summoned Annie from the kitchen, a wooden horse that swung from ropes while the rider swatted at a tethered croquet ball. I could have done worse than follow his male example. And George must have liked me well enough. He built me a model airplane, the old-fashioned kind made out of tissue paper and bits of balsa wood, cut out with a razor blade and glued together. But George's character was marred by grave flaws, hinted at darkly by my mother but not to be explained to children.

The local public school stood just on the other side of our brook, no more than a mile away if you cut through the woods, and the school bus ran right by our door, but it was not to be contemplated that we would go to public school with the farmers' children. My oldest sister attended a fashionable boarding school that she loathed. My middle sister, always specially favored by fate and my parents, was permitted to ride into New Haven every day to private school. My youngest sister and I remained at home to be taught by my mother.

It was not a happy arrangement. My mother has never been comfortable with little boys, although she can be charming with little girls. Thirty years later, I sat entranced as she told stories to my own daughter and illustrated them with pencil sketches executed on the spot. But she bullied and ridiculed my son, who hated her in return. She used to do the same to me, partly from ignorance of males (having grown up without brothers and in a rigidly Victorian household) and partly because she believed in a gentleman's code composed in equal parts of King Arthur's Round Table, Louisa May Alcott, and the Pauline epistles and imposed on any male children unlucky enough to toddle within her dominion.

She was particularly rigorous with me after Cathy left, and in my first-grade lessons she gave me to understand that I must look not to God but to her for mercy. How I dreaded those lessons! Each began with her irritation and my uneasiness, and accelerated swiftly into rage on her part and paralysis on mine. If I read "cow" when the book said "farmer," her anger rose. I would stumble from word to word, and her fury would mount at each mistake until my words became soggy with tears. To this day, I read at half normal speed, sounding each word cautiously to myself before moving on to the next.

But as compensation I had the joy of art periods, a pleasure not because I liked working with clay and paints, which I did not, but because I was permitted to wear a dress—a blue-and-white pinafore, discarded by one of my sisters and intended as an apron to protect my clothes. I insisted, however, on removing my boy's clothing before putting on the pinafore, and when art period ended, I fought against changing back again. Occasionally, by dint of tears and tantrums, I was allowed to wear the pinafore until bedtime. In those blissful hours, I reveled in the joy and freedom of temporarily being a girl, though I was too wary of punishment and ridicule to reveal that pleasure. I knew that my mother would confiscate my dress if she discovered how much I cherished it. (In my mother's defense, I do not believe she understood the sexual implications of that pinafore. Some transsexual case histories cite mothers who perversely dress their sons as girls, but I doubt that many women are silly enough to imperil a boy's gender identity in this way. In any event, my sense of femaleness was already well-developed before I ever put on that pinafore.)

Soon disaster began to overtake us in a variety of forms. My maternal grandfather, whom I adored, died of heart disease after a long and excruciating illness. My father followed him a few months later, dead in an instant when he piled his three-week-old Ford roadster into a concrete bridge abutment. The *New Haven Register* hinted broadly that he was drunk at the time. Then the stock market crash wiped us out financially.

After my father's life insurance had been used to pay off the mortgage, we had little left but my maternal grandmother's charity and my mother's pride. My mother closed our country house and moved us into a house in New Haven, loaned to us rent-free by university friends. She ran classified ads in the *Register*, seeking work as a cleaning woman, but banks and factories were closing and no one was hiring servants. In the face of all reason, however, we clung to our own servants. George and Annie were installed in a maid's room of our cavernous, borrowed house, and Annie went on making applesauce cake as if nothing had happened. George, with virtually no grounds and only one remaining car to maintain, took a job in a factory making railroad wheels. But exposed to the temptations of the city,

George now showed what my mother had hinted at as the darker side of his character. He was, it appeared, a drinker. So more in sorrow than in anger—though in just a bit of anger too, I suspect—my mother discharged them both. Out of revenge, George drove to our country house, now shuttered for the winter, and dismantled all his inventions. Not one of them ever worked again. Many years later, we read in the *Register* that he had been killed by a hit-and-run driver while changing a tire for a stranger on Route 1, not ten miles from the house he first had served and later vandalized.

Remembering the event today, I believe my mother fired George and Annie less in outrage than from necessity. We were maintaining the façade of affluence, but now our clothes, though still bearing the labels of Best's and De-Pinna's, came to us secondhand from more fortunate friends and cousins. We attended private schools but on scholarships. Since nothing in our past had prepared her for such economic straits, my mother determined to prepare herself by enrolling in secretarial school. She never penetrated the mysteries of Pitman shorthand, but she did conquer the typewriter and went to work as a secretary at the university, where she doggedly remained for many years.

Transsexuals are often said to have enjoyed warm, often deplorably intimate relationships with their mothers. (Psychologists have recorded case histories of mothers who fondled their sons in a shockingly unmaternal way, bathed with them, and slept nude in the same bed while relegating the father to another room.) In this respect, I do not fit the classic mold. I found my mother cold and critical. Yet I also found her unequaled for competence and courage. These are usually thought of as masculine virtues, but I learned them from a woman. When at last I began to turn into a woman myself, I resolved that I would not become one of those capricious and helpless nitwits so often held up as the American standard.

The fact that women are different from men was relentlessly hammered home during my childhood, and in every difference it seemed that women held a clear advantage. As the sole surviving male in the family, I bore certain obligations from which my sisters were free. I was required to mow the lawn, surrender my seat in a bus, fetch reading glasses and Kleenexes, wait at doors, hold chairs at the dining table, and carry steamer trunks up to the attic. None of this, however, was to be construed as excusing me from doing my "fair share around the house." I was obliged to make my bed, vacuum the house, set and clear the table, and either wash or dry the dishes, all on equal terms with my sisters. On those occasions when they were "feeling under the weather," my portion of these chores became somewhat more than equal. Under no circumstances was I permitted to hit them, because girls were said to be fragile and easily broken. In truth, they were far bigger than I and often hit me with impunity, and I festered with the injustice of being forbidden to defend myself.

My mother and my youngest sister together constituted a sort of feminist league devoted to ridicule of male conduct and disgust at male appetites. As a male I was, by definition, excluded from their deliberations, though secretly I felt no more kinship with men than they did. (Over the years I have admired men and enjoyed their company, but always knowing that I was not like them.) But neither could I be admitted to the society of women, where I felt I belonged. The typical transsexual case history speaks of a childhood preference for playing with girls rather than boys. I, too, would have preferred this, but experience taught me that girls do not welcome boys into their games and confidences. I was an outcast, ineligible to enter the female world and unable to enter the male.

Still my mother hounded me toward manhood, continually preaching her ideal of manly conduct, the salient features of which were sacrifice, loyalty, industry, thrift, conservatism, and courage in the face of pain. As a woman, my mother was not obligated to honor this code herself but merely to inform me of its specifications. My father, she testified, had observed it all diligently, an assertion I came to regard with rising skepticism over the years. No man since Robert E. Lee could have conducted himself with such comprehensive, unflagging nobility. Certainly I couldn't, though I tried.

At the age of nine, I was sent off to summer camp to "learn to be a man." The upper middle class still used phrases like that and believed them too. There appeared to be no feminine corollary to "learning to be a man." Girls just naturally grew up to be women without any formal instruction, but men were to be hammered into the required shape on the anvil of discipline and hardship. That had long been the custom on both sides of the family, in which most of the men had been military officers. My father had entered the Naval Academy at the age of sixteen (he resigned after a year, just before they threw him out for sloppiness and insubordination, though he later fought with distinction as an infantry officer in the trenches of World War I); one of my great-grandfathers, a Civil War cavalry general, fell on the field of battle, nobly according to family legend, ignobly according to eyewitness accounts; and another great-grandfather, as a sixteen-year-old midshipman, shot his first man while leading a landing party at Vera Cruz—his victim, one of his own boat crew, had tried to desert the instant the boat touched shore; so my great-grandfather plugged him in the leg.

The camp to which I was dispatched lay on a rocky inlet on the Maine coast and smelled of evergreens and the sea. Like most such institutions, it had a dining hall, sleeping cabins, a crafts shop, a fleet of canoes, a swimming float, and a few small sailboats. Transsexuals typically abhor sports and all forms of "rough and tumble" (Renee Richards being a notable exception), and I contrived to avoid tennis and baseball, though I did learn to shoot a .22 rifle, row a boat, and swim a passable crawl. And most of all I learned to sail. Every hour I could arrange it, I spent in the clinker-built Cape Cod knockabouts, beating out into Montsweag Bay. A love affair with sailboats would obsess me for the next thirty years.

My competence in small boats helped save me from ostracism. My cabinmates sensed my difference, perhaps because of the hours I spent alone, lying on my bunk and playing my harmonica, perhaps because of the subtly feminine cast of my conversation, acquired through long immersion in a totally feminine household. I was shocked to see their naked bodies and ashamed to show them mine. Their attachment to baseball mystified me. Their language appalled me. None of us had yet embarked upon puberty, so their maleness sprang more from training and instinct than from open sexuality, but already at nine years old they were well advanced on the road to manhood while I trailed reluctantly and at a distance. I did not understand them, I did not like the things they liked, I did not want to emulate them. Most of all, I didn't want to fight them. I was a wretched wrestler and a worse boxer, easily tripped, ignorant of the hammerlock, wide open to any haymaker. These are vital arts to little boys, who spend a vast amount of time fighting, and I was inept in all of them. Miraculously, my vulnerability was seldom revealed. Slyly but fervently I avoided combat with my peers. Indeed I often made them laugh. Perhaps they sympathized with my softness because they had only recently become hard themselves and sometimes longed for the old, easier times. Occasionally some oaf would smell out my hidden effeminacy and try to bully me, but a champion would unfailingly rise to my defense. I seldom had to fight for myself.

I would spend almost every day in the sailboats, at first as a neophyte, later frequently as a surrogate instructor. Here I found my natural element and exceeded the others, who hesitated to condemn someone who sailed as well as I did.

Each summer the camp produced a Gilbert and Sullivan operetta, alternately *The Pirates of Penzance* and *H.M.S. Pinafore*. Both required choruses of maidens, recruited from among the campers like the rest of the cast. How I yearned to be cast as a maiden, dressed in bonnet and long skirt. I prayed to God each morning after breakfast as I walked to the latrine to please, please make me a maiden, and I cursed God and the director when I was designated a pirate the first summer and a sailor the second. It didn't matter that I craved to be a girl, if only briefly in a play. God's will had been revealed to me, and I had better bow my neck to the yoke of masculinity.

To complete my education in manhood, I was shipped off to prep school at the age of twelve. And to allow the staff sufficient time to whip me into the required shape, I started not as a freshman but as an eighth-grader, thus condemned to serve five years in that harsh institution, that shrine of emergent virility.

The red-brick dormitories and classroom buildings of Pomfret were strung out along the ridge of a hill where the cruel winds of winter could lash each one impartially. As January followed in the frozen tracks of December, the cold deepened, the drifts of snow rose higher, and darkness fell earlier and earlier.

My heart lay as bleak as the landscape. Again my peers smelled out my difference, but now no champion arose to defend me, the perils of chivalry being disproportionate to the rewards in that school where unpopular causes were censured and eccentricity was punished. If I chose to avoid football, shun the gymnasium, mock the cherished rituals of the Saturday game, then I must be punished too. I never received a copy of the indictment for which I was made to stand trial over the next two years, but I suppose the charges must have included my sarcasm, which really was intolerable, my abhorrence of the jockstrap society, and my disregard for male values, a failing that stemmed more from incapacity than from deliberate contempt.

Although the penalties contrived for me by my schoolmates lacked imagination, they did achieve impact through repetition. My room would be endlessly ransacked, my belongings strewn about, my books thrown from their shelves, my strongbox jimmied. In the train on the way to school, I would be tripped, sent sprawling, my typewriter crashing—broken—at my head. In the dining hall line I would be punched in the kidney, and when I looked around no one would be brave enough to accept responsibility, though every face wore a conspiratorial smirk. No act of hostility was too petty. If I left my coat on a hook, they searched the pockets, tore my notebook in half, and broke my mechanical pencil. I shall never forget the incredulous horror of finding that notebook and pencil destroyed, of knowing that some classmate—and I would never learn who—bore me such malice.

Each morning after breakfast, the entire student body assembled in the high-ceilinged study hall with its varnished wainscoting, its sepia pictures of Roman ruins, and its stuffed mooseheads staring balefully down from the walls. The headmaster would stand before us on the dais, shaggy with tweed, redolent of cigars, and deliver ten-minute homilies on manliness and honor. I learned much of manliness and honor at his school.

To my astonishment, my second year I fought them off, even beat them in a sense. I recall the night the tide turned. The moment came a few minutes after lights-out when the customary gang of vigilantes burst into my room, shouting and laughing. Again I felt the cold fear in my stomach, though I dared not show it because fear heightened their fury as spilled blood will stir a pack of sharks to frenzy. But to my dazed relief, they had come not for me but for my roommate. They threw him bodily against the wall, lashed him with their belts, hit him with their fists, and finally soaked him and his bed with a wastebasketful of water. Then they left him weeping in his sodden bed. I regarded his huddled, shaking form with contempt. They had done the same and worse to me on other nights, but they had never made me cry. Not aloud. And yet I could not rest comfortably. I had not hit him myself, but neither had I tried to save him. I dared not. Even as I rejoiced that I had been spared, I drowned in shame.

But I did not let my shame prevent me from enjoying the

friendship they now offered me as capriciously as they had formerly withheld it. Neither did I understand why my condemnation had been lifted. I still abhorred their sports, their baseball statistics, their jockstraps (sometimes dangling comically from the ceiling light fixtures of their rooms). I knew that I had not changed, though often enough I would have utterly transformed myself to escape their persecutions if only I had known how. In subsequent flights of fancy, I have played with the hypothesis that it was they who had changed, not I, that my resistance in the face of all their horror at last touched some chord of rising sympathy.

Whatever the reason, I was finally accepted, and for that benison I willingly suspended my own honor and pride. When the Drama Club produced *Arsenic and Old Lace*, I played the nutty brother who thinks he's Teddy Roosevelt at San Juan Hill and dashes up the stairs, alternately blowing a bugle and crying, "Charge!" They thumped me on the back in congratulations and said admiringly that they hadn't known I had it in me. I became the class wit, delegated to write all the satirical skits and class notes. By the day I graduated, I had achieved the status of a minor celebrity. More than that, I had survived the annealing fires of manhood.

And I had defied them. Through all those bitter years, each night as I lay in the dark and listened to the distant train whistle, I dreamed of being a girl, free of the barbarous demands of masculinity. I knew well enough that I was not a girl—I had only to look at what my body had become: five feet ten inches tall, skinny as a fence post, muscles hard, beard growing, hair sprouting on chest and stomach. Secret dreams aside, I was locked in an undoubtedly male body, and like most adolescent male bodies it was bubbling with hormones and potent as a cocked pistol. For this condition, there could be little relief aside from masturbation, which we all practiced intemperately. My mother's chivalric code forbade sexual intercourse outside marriage, and besides, in that monastic school there was no opportunity aside from sodomy, an indulgence that has always struck me as incomprehensible. We saw girls on vacations, but I doubt that few if any of my classmates got laid during their Pomfret years. They nonetheless talked knowingly and perpetually about it, and I learned to participate in these discussions. Occasionally I even dated girls myself and always I was feverishly interested in them. I studied their hair, their clothes, their figures. And I brooded about the increasing differences between us. I seethed with envy while at the same time becoming sexually aroused—I wanted to possess them even as I wanted to become them. In my nighttime fantasies, as I masturbated or floated toward sleep, I combined the two compulsions, dreaming of sex but with myself as the girl, my partner blanked out because I so loathed the male body, even my own.

World War II was entering its final spring as graduation neared. For almost four years, the school had shuddered in the winds of war. The headmaster had wangled a major's commission and gone off to do his part in Washington. The draft had nibbled away at the faculty and gobbled up most of the recent graduates. At Sunday services, the school chaplain would read the names of the latest casualties, Pomfret boys who had died at Guadalcanal and Tarawa, at Omaha Beach and St. Lo.

In June 1945 my turn came. Like my classmates, I had given a good deal of thought to how I would serve my country. Those with 20/20 eyesight had signed up for air cadet or other officer candidate programs, but I was exceedingly

nearsighted and hence ineligible despite heroic doses of vita-
min pills and a regimen of eye exercises. The Navy and mer-
chant marine had already rejected me, and I doubted that I
could pass the Army eye test either. It was possible to become an ambulance driver with the British forces, but I was
determined to prove myself the equal of my classmates, and
so when I took the Army physical, I memorized the eye
chart. They made me an infantry rifleman.

With a few hundred other New England draftees, I was
put in Army fatigues, Army boots, and Army underwear,
and shipped in a troop train to Fort McClellan, Alabama,
for basic training. For seventeen weeks we lived in tar-paper
huts drawn up in ranks on either side of the powder-dirt
company street. At one end of the street stood company
headquarters and the latrine, at the other the mess hall and a
full-length mirror on whose frame were printed the words *I
am a tough, rugged, fighting Infantryman.* At first when I
studied my reflection—hollow-chested, stoop-shouldered—
I laughed self-consciously, but before the training cycle had
ended, I believed the mirror's words. I had been taught feats
I had previously considered impossible: I could march
twenty-two miles with a full field pack and an M-1 rifle,
carry a 60-mm mortar up a mountain, chin myself fifty times
with my hands the wrong way around on the bar, perform a
hundred push-ups and then another hundred as punishment
because I had laughed. I could, in theory, kill a man with
any one of seventeen weapons, including the hand grenade,
the .30-caliber light machine gun (air-cooled), and the bayonet. Now when I studied myself in the company mirror, I
thought I saw a tough, dangerous, competent man. The military uniform always bolstered my masculine self-image, a
fact that I suspect holds true for many men.

I enjoyed that summer in the murderous Alabama heat, crawling about on my stomach amid the rattlesnakes, under a hail of machine-gun fire and artillery shells, all quite genuine. I enjoyed playing soldier, strutting about the post in starched khakis, popping salutes to the officers. I gloried in the health and vigor of my new strength. I delighted in the acceptance of my platoonmates, none of whom had had a nurse or gone to prep school. And for two blissful years of Army service I believed I had established my credentials as a man among men. I cherished this belief even as, night after night, lying on my iron cot, I dreamed of being a girl.

The war ended before I had completed basic training, a circumstance that undoubtedly saved my life since, despite my military posturing, I lacked that killer instinct which protects a rifleman in combat. On the day Japan surrendered in August 1945, we were climbing up and down cargo nets and attacking a mock Japanese village in preparation for the final assault on the home islands.

But instead of an invasion we had a victory parade. Every able-bodied man in Fort McClellan fell out in Class B uniform with rifle, bayonet, and helmet, and marched to the vast parade ground. By the time my company arrived, the ground was nearly half full. For an hour and more we stood at parade rest while rivers of men flowed in through four approaches—thousands upon thousands of young riflemen, marching four abreast to the blare of an Army band. When all the troops had been assembled, we swung past the reviewing stand at eyes right while our officers saluted a covey of generals, the flags and guidons whipped in the breeze, and a hundred thousand boots pounded the ground in rhythm with the brazen trumpets.

But victory did not free us from the Army. While combat

veterans were returning from overseas, I shipped out of New York harbor on a troop transport, out past the Statue of Liberty, past a grassy bank on which the words *Welcome Home* had been spelled with whitewashed boulders, out onto the North Atlantic, lashed white by November gales. They put me ashore in Newfoundland, where I was eventually promoted to sergeant and put in charge of a string of warehouses and eleven men.

Most of my men were Newfoundland civilians old enough to be my grandfather. A few were soldiers like me, and of these one was a tough kid named Krause from the slums of Philadelphia. The others were compliant enough as long as I didn't drive them too hard, but Krause took a dim view of discipline, especially when I imposed it. He slept on duty atop a pile of mattresses in the back of the main warehouse, disappeared entirely from sight for hours at a time, and lied about his work. No word of mine could inspire his better nature. Baffled, I reported him at last to my boss, Master Sergeant Virgil Potts, a tall and courtly Virginian who wore his authority with natural grace along with a thin line of mustache that I was trying to emulate. Sergeant Potts, I knew, could eat Krause for breakfast and never even burp.

Krause was white-lipped with rage.

"If you wasn't a sergeant," he fumed, "I'd take you out behind the warehouse and beat the shit out of you!"

We were standing outside my office in the gloom of the great warehouse, surrounded by my men, who like Krause had just returned from lunch. All my white-haired civilian laborers were there, ruminating on their foul-smelling pipes. They had an agreeable habit of observing—whenever I was near enough to overhear—that "you've got to get up early in the morning, boy, to fool Sergeant Hunt!" (The word *boy* was pronounced as if it were spelled "buy.") I knew they would no longer utter that fawning sentiment if I permitted Krause to intimidate me. Sergeant George Riggins was there, the Georgia swamp rat whom I had supplanted in the section and whose office I had taken over. I imagined that Riggins would enjoy seeing my face bloodied.

None of them would ever obey me again if I retreated now from Krause. Yet he sprang from a far tougher world than mine, a world of alley fights and broken bottles. I knew the ground behind the warehouse. It was steeply sloped and covered with sharp outcroppings and razorlike shards of rock. I would be badly hurt. My heart blocked my throat and filled my chest with its pounding. So great was my fear and so dry my mouth that I could scarcely speak.

"All right, Krause," I croaked, struggling to steady my voice, "I'll go out behind the warehouse with you."

"Yeah, you'd like that, wouldn't you," Krause sneered. "You get me to hit a sergeant, and then you get me court-martialed."

"You won't be court-martialed," I said. "I'll take off my shirt and leave my stripes in the office."

For long seconds we glared at each other, white-faced, and the other men stared silently at us. I knew I was scared. Perhaps Krause was too.

Presently he dropped his eyes from mine, and I knew that I had won. "Argh, I'm not going to fight you," he snarled, and he turned and left the warehouse. Slowly my pulse and respiration began to subside.

That night in the NCO club, I became very drunk indeed, and in that condition I fell into conversation with Sergeant Riggins. "I was so scared," I confessed. "I knew that if he got me out behind the warehouse, he was going to kill me."

Riggins laughed. "You didn't have no cause to worry, Sergeant," he said, "because I was going out there with you. And if he'd laid a hand on you, I was going to tear his head off."

I was immensely proud of my rank as buck sergeant. To me those chevrons on my sleeves symbolized my membership in the community of men, my acceptance by Riggins and Potts and all the other soldiers whose self-assured virility I so much envied. To this day, I secretly celebrate the anniversary of my promotion to sergeant on August 12, 1946, though I have long since forgotten the dates of my college graduation, my two weddings, and my children's birthdays.

I was tempted to stay in the Army, but a career as an enlisted man would have fallen short of my mother's expectations for me, and at the age of nineteen I felt compelled to go home and start college. In the troopship that carried me back to New York harbor, I found myself the ranking noncommissioned officer, nominally in charge of two hundred troops, most of them miserably seasick. Stacked four-deep in their pipe berths, they threw up on themselves and each other as they lay stewing in the reek of their own filth. For the last time, I exerted myself as a leader of men, hounding some of them up on deck into the open air, bathing others, organizing work details to mop the vomit from the decks. Again the North Atlantic had caught me in November, and the ship rolled like a drunken whore. I have never been seasick, although I came near it that week, down in the stench of those crowded berthing spaces. But I was never so happy as while nursing those sick and helpless guys.

My military adventures behind me, I walked up the concrete ramp of the New Haven railroad station with my duffel bag on my shoulder. At the top of the incline my mother awaited me, as she had so often when I returned from boarding school for vacations, slightly aggrieved at having had to fetch me, usually disapproving of some shortcoming in my appearance. My mother considered melodrama in bad taste, and she felt disinclined to play a scene with me from *The Hero's Return*. We embraced ritually, and I saw her, as I had known I would, contemptuously examining my mustache, which I had trimmed to a thin line in emulation of Master Sergeant Potts. As mustaches went it was a puny, adolescent effort, not at all to be compared with my father's exuberant growth. I seemed condemned always to have my own pretentions to manhood weighed against my father's achievements—weighed and found wanting. Of course, my father had been dead for many years, and I was competing with a mythological ideal deified on the altar of my mother's memory. It was an impossible game to beat. In my mind's eye, I could see the chevrons being ripped from my sleeves, the brass buttons cut from my uniform, the campaign ribbons torn from my chest and ground disdainfully beneath my mother's heel on the concrete ramp of the New Haven railroad station.

We drove out to the white clapboard house in the country where my mother had returned to live year-round as soon as I had been safely dispatched to boarding school. Delightedly I prowled the rooms I loved so well, my eyes and hands caressing the books in the library, the white ruffled curtains in every window, the simple beauty of the fireplace carvings, a row of luster pitchers, fragile and glowing with a dark, coppery loveliness, the silver candlesticks, an arrangement of bittersweet in a pewter tankard, a glass-walled Tiffany clock. The hard angularity of the barracks had vanished, and I was sinking, at once gratefully and reluctantly, into the feminine comforts of home. Aside from my duffel bag upstairs in my bedroom, I could find nothing to link my present with my past, not even the one symbol I had always felt certain had marked my absence. I looked at the living room windows, then crossed the front hall and looked in the library. No, there was nothing. It had been the custom during World War II, as it had in World War I, to hang a service flag in the front window when a member of the family entered the armed forces, with a blue star on a white field for each son or father who had been called. If the son or father were killed, the blue star was replaced with gold. Many houses displayed these flags, often with three or four stars. My mother had showed one for my father during World War I, but she had none for me. My Army service was not to be compared with my father's. It might almost never have existed.

I entered Yale two months later in the winter term. Mine was the largest class in the history of the university, 1,750 of us at the beginning and 1,500 at the end, about half veterans. We all wore old uniforms to class: naval officers' bridge coats, infantrymen's field jackets, fleece-lined flight jackets, uniform shirts, many still bearing the marks of recently removed chevrons or the rust-stained holes where officers' bars had been pinned. Those who had not legitimately acquired such garments on the field of honor bought them at Army surplus stores. In those early postwar years, the university looked like a training camp.

Like the rest, I wore the remnants of my uniform, clinging to the fiction of a virile world that I had in fact lost. I relished every opportunity to exchange war stories with my classmates. A former lieutenant colonel lived across the hall from me and a winner of the Bronze Star roomed downstairs. My instructor in Greek drama had fought with the OSS, sneaking about behind the German lines and blowing up railroad bridges. I bought my first car from a P-47 fighter pilot and eventually sold it to the co-pilot of an RAF Lancaster bomber. In English history class, my instructor (naval air intelligence) explained the Battle of Agincourt, after which I compared it with modern infantry tactics, assisted by the student who sat beside me, a disabled Marine Corps company commander. Every Saturday night, my roommate and I played bridge with a P-38 fighter pilot and his wife. I associated almost exclusively with veterans, attempting to extend the manly triumph of my Army career.

But sometimes, finding the white clapboard house empty, I rifled my sisters' bureau drawers and closets, finding a girdle here, a pair of stockings there, a dress that I knew would fit, a scarf, a lipstick. I would dress as a woman and gaze at my reflection in my mother's bedroom mirror. That lean, hard body, that male face stained with the blue shadow of beard, decked out in nylons and ruffles! It was obscene, ludicrous, disgusting. The incongruity could never be repaired. I could never be a woman, no matter how passionately I wished it. My body would grow paunchy and bald and hairy, my complexion would coarsen, my face would become craggy and seamed as the years of maleness seared me ever more deeply. I was condemned to perpetual imprisonment in that loathsome frame. Unspeakably saddened, I took off my sisters' clothes and restored them to closet and bureau drawer, taking care to leave them precisely as I had found them so that no one would ever suspect my hateful secret.

Even I did not understand that secret. Never having heard of transsexualism, I supposed I must be a homosexual, and the thought sickened me. For years in dormitories and barracks I had lived among male bodies, and they appalled me. In the shower room I averted my eyes. At the urinal I could not perform in the presence of anyone else but had to sit on the toilet and void like a girl. To contemplate homosexuality, to imagine the embrace of sinewy arms and hairy legs so like my own, dismayed me.

Dazed with self-absorption and disgust, I moved through the university without seeing or hearing. I would read sixty pages of *War and Peace* and realize that I had not understood a word, and I would have to do it all again. In the classroom, lectures droned on about my ears for fifty minutes at a time while I sat impervious, wrapped in my preoccupations.

I had thought to study civil engineering at Yale. I imagined myself in riding breeches and pith helmet, peering through a transit in the Amazon jungle, while above me towered the concrete bluffs of the hydraulic dam that I was building. I can't think why I should have wanted to wear riding breeches in the Amazon jungle—I just always pictured the scene that way. But an aptitude test revealed my unsuitability for the science of engineering, and so I became an English major. I did not know exactly what I might do with my knowledge of English literature. I didn't want to teach it, since that would require graduate school and I wasn't even sure I could make it through college. I thought myself too stupid. So when at length I received my degree, I was greatly surprised and relieved. I had graduated precisely in the middle of my class.

I had no notion of what to do with my life now except that, like most graduates who have majored in English, I thought I might go to New York and try my hand at book publishing. But not right away. At a graduation reception, two friends invited me to accompany them to Europe and crew for them in a series of sailboat races. That struck me as a good idea, but my mother, who was present, grimly vetoed it on the grounds that I should look for a job and begin my life's work, whatever it was to be. I was then twenty-three years old and an Army veteran, but I submitted to her will.

I moved back into my old bedroom in the white clapboard house and began a desultory search for a job in book publishing. Occasionally I would overcome my lassitude sufficiently to take the train down to New York and join the bright-faced new graduates camped in publishers' waiting rooms. But I didn't really want to work there, and the publishers didn't really want to hire me. I didn't read their books, I cared nothing for their authors, and I knew little about the literary marketplace, even less about the mechanics of book production.

As the summer passed, I went less often to New York and instead spent the days reading and walking the paths that threaded the woods for miles about the house. Sometimes, if my mother had not already preceded me there, I would drive up to Maine and stay with my aunt. The house there was rooted to a granite ledge whose gnarled fingers reached out into the sea. By day I scrambled over the rocks and gazed into the salty pools at the starfish and scuttling hermit crabs. By night I lay and listened to the clangor of the bell buoy that marked the entrance to the harbor half a mile down the coast. Sometimes a great storm rolled in from the northeast, and the waves hurled themselves upon the rocks in towering rage so that the earth's granite foundation seemed to tremble beneath their blows. My aunt, a woman of far greater wit and intelligence than my own, accepted me uncritically, and alone with her in that ocean house my sense of unworthiness receded. (Curiously, my aunt, in all other respects a woman of remarkable perception, clung to the belief that I was antifeminist or what would later be called "a male chauvinist pig.")

From this lotus land the Pentagon summoned me once more. As a last link with the profession of arms, I had retained my membership in the Reserves, a hedge against the day of Armageddon, and though the Korean War did not rank with Armageddon, it did require my services at an Air Force base outside San Antonio.

But by this time the military life had lost its power to assure me of my manhood. Kelly Air Force Base was a world of clerk-typists. No machine-gun fire rattled over my head, no red-faced cadreman led me through the rigors of bayonet drill, no band played for me on the parade ground. The war impinged on me only when I saw the great C-97s touch down on the runway outside my barracks window at the end of the long air-evac route from Korea. The airplane doors would open and the litter-bearers would bring forth the wounded on stretchers. When the last casualties had been stowed away in the ambulances, only the flight nurses remained, standing in blood-stained coveralls beside the aircraft, blinking in the sun like the exhausted survivors of a catastrophe.

Because I had been a supply sergeant in the previous war, they set me to work in a warehouse, issuing the Air Force's recently adopted blue uniform. My special task was to measure the height of each man's crotch from the floor. I endured this for three days before going to the personnel officer and protesting, "Look, you can't do this to me; I'm a Yale graduate." He was a reasonable man, and so he made me an education specialist, charged with peddling corre- spondence courses and administering intelligence tests. It wasn't a soldier's job, and I felt like neither a soldier nor a man. I slouched about the base with my shoulders bowed and my hands in my pockets. When retreat sounded for the lowering of the colors each evening, I ran for the shelter of the nearest building rather than stand at hand salute, some- thing I had once done with pride. The only officers I will- ingly saluted were the flight nurses, those tired, bloodied women who had seen too much.

When at the end of a year the Air Force let me depart, I returned to my mother and resumed my reading and my walks in the woods. I knew now that the military life was a delusion, but I had no other. And so, because I didn't know what to do with myself, I looked about for someone to tell me and presently found the guidance counselor who gave me the Guilford-Zimmerman gender test, among a dozen others. Having announced that I had the mind of a woman, he suggested that I become a librarian—significantly, I re- alized later, a profession dominated by women. I might have done well to heed his advice; after all, I'd paid thirty-five dollars for it. Indeed, I did go down to Columbia University and enroll in its School of Library Service, but I never began classes. Instead, I turned my face resolutely in another di- rection and set out once more to prove myself a man.

FIVE

The road to successful manhood, I decided, lay through the thickets of business. This notion was founded shakily on a supposition that commerce must be an easy game, considering some of the nitwits I knew who had made their fortunes in it. So I found a job as a sort of shipping expediter in a New Haven concern whose chief distinction lay in the fact that it was the world's largest manufacturer of douche bags. It made a lot of other products, including enema bags, colostomy bags, and hot water bags—anything that could be fabricated from rubber.

A few of the executives considered me a promising young man, and they allowed me to come within striking distance of my own glass-walled office with my own secretary and dictaphone, but at the last minute these prizes were awarded to a more qualified candidate. So I did the logical thing—I quit. I would not have remained happy there in any event; increasingly I had come to doubt whether I wanted to devote my life to the douche-bag industry.

Accepting what I considered my destiny, I arranged to

enter Columbia University's library school and cast about for a temporary job to sustain me until I could begin the next academic term in February. It was then November, and I would soon need money for Christmas presents. Two possibilities occurred to me: I could go to the New Haven Post Office, where they were hiring help for the Christmas rush, or I could go down to our village green and ask for a job on the local weekly newspaper. Reluctant to face the daily drive into New Haven, I chose the weekly newspaper and was hired there as an apprentice printer for forty dollars a week.

I have worked on newspapers ever since. Not that I intended to do so, my guidance counselor having told me dogmatically that I could never stand the deadline pressures. He was right, in a sense. I have faced deadlines every working day of my life and have never been able to abide them.

The offices of that weekly newspaper might have sprung from Dickens. Almost every typewriter and printing press and case of type dated from the Victorian or Edwardian era. Nothing had been added except the years' accumulation of scrap paper and grime. In this dingy, ill-lit world I found a semblance of happiness for the first time since I had left the Army. I learned to set headlines, cast advertising stereotype plates, make up pages, and run the old flatbed newspaper press.

I was working in that newspaper shop in 1952 when the New York *Daily News* broke the story of Christine Jorgensen. The front page was entirely occupied by the headline and picture of the ex-GI who had become a blonde beauty— an ex-GI like me. My family read only the *New York Times,* and I didn't buy the *Daily News* myself, but I furtively borrowed any copy I could find lying about the shop and read and reread the stories, both that first day and for the next few weeks before the tabloids grew bored with it all. So great were my interest and envy that my heartbeat accelerated and my vision blurred as I read.

No news event has ever shaken me like the Christine Jorgensen story. Other transsexuals were similarly affected, I later learned. The poor woman was inundated with desperate letters. But there was still no practical help for any of us. Yes, it had been demonstrated that an anatomical male could be converted into a facsimile of a female, but only in a foreign country and only on an experimental basis. American doctors, I felt certain, would never undertake such a scandalous procedure. The law would not permit it. Society would not condone it. And most of all, my mother would forever stand in my way.

When the day came to begin my studies at Columbia, I went to work as usual at the printing shop. I had come to like working on a weekly newspaper, and after it became apparent that I would never learn to be a printer, my pay was raised to fifty dollars a week and I was appointed editor of a smaller weekly owned by the same company. I might be there yet if I hadn't fallen into the habit of arguing with the publisher, a wealthy retired lawyer with a shrewd sense of business. He tolerated my impertinence for longer than I had a right to expect, and then one evening he called me out to his car and fired me.

Though I had no journalistic training except the little I had acquired by eight months' observation, I could not conceive of working anywhere but on a newspaper. So I presented myself in the city room of the *New Haven Register,* whose circulation of 100,000 was somewhat more than 100 times as large as that of the paper from which I had just been fired.

"I guess I could use you as a copy editor," said the managing editor, a choleric, red-faced Irishman.

"That's great!" I said enthusiastically. "What's a copy editor?"

He looked pained, but he hired me anyway at sixty dollars a week, a ten-dollar improvement over my last position, and told me to report at 6:00 A.M. the next morning. I learned soon enough what a copy editor is: a clerical drudge who sits tied to his desk like a galley slave chained to his bench, editing news stories at top speed like a demented English teacher correcting essays, repairing grammar, fixing misspellings, and remedying major misstatements of fact. For each story he also writes a headline, which must fit the allotted space and bear a passing resemblance to the content of the article. Next to working on an assembly line, it is the most tedious and harassing work I know, and I was to do it for many years.

Newspaper city rooms ranked then with the locker rooms of professional football teams among the great bastions of masculinity. Aside from the four members of the society department, the woman who wrote the fashion column, and a couple of reporters who covered some of the suburban beats, we had no women on the editorial staff. I did not encounter a woman copy editor for eight years. (According to then-prevailing newspaper lore, women were tone-deaf to double entendres and might allow salacious ones to sneak into the paper.)

I drew comfort from the hearty environment of the city room and felt myself to be a man among men, much as I had felt in the Army. I used liquor and profanity immoderately. I kept my hair mowed short in a quarter-inch crew cut, a style I had picked up in basic training and clung to until, many years later, I began to cultivate the tresses appropriate to womanhood. I dated an adorable little flibbertigibbet named Doris who imposed no great burden on either my intellect or my uncertain sexuality. And I continued to live in the white clapboard house, which I shared only with my mother, all my sisters having left to establish homes of their own.

I had a small sailing dinghy that I kept on a saltwater mooring a few miles away, and to satisfy my softer yearnings I began to take piano lessons. The piano appealed to me, and I began to study it passionately, as later, in a different life and a different sex, I was to throw myself into flying light airplanes. Because I was single and had no responsibilities apart from my job, I could devote enormous blocks of time to the piano—two lessons a week and four hours of practice a day, sometimes five or six on my days off. I could practice Hanon exercises for an entire morning and never lose interest or the sense of wonder that my fingers could perform these coordinated intricacies. I committed pages and pages of Bach and Chopin to memory. By the end of the second year, my piano teacher and I were discussing the possibility of my entering the Yale School of Music.

Twenty-nine years old and still living at home with my mother, I had begun to wonder what was the matter with me. Doris's enchanting mannerisms were starting to drive me to distraction and we fought frequently. Continuing to fantasize about being a woman, I remained a male virgin. In that depressing situation, marriage seemed a likely way to gain approval as a male and as a human being. To prove my claim, at the age of twenty-nine, I married a girl from the *Register*'s society department.

My bride was a slim and poignant beauty with dark, doe-like eyes and an ineffable grace of movement. She also had a tongue that could skin the bark off a tree, though I didn't realize it until we had been married for several months. I used to watch her floating down the stairs to the city room from the morgue, two steps at a time, her full skirt swirling about her knees. I thought myself blessed to have won her. We were married on the Saturday of the Yale-Harvard football game.

I had chosen my bride by a process of calculation. I knew that she had risen from lower-class poverty, had won a scholarship to a first-rate women's college, and had been elected to Phi Beta Kappa in her junior year. She had chosen to work in the hard-boiled world of newspapers. On this scanty evidence, I concluded that she was an achiever, a climber with whom I could conquer the world. Instead she became a millstone, unsupportive of my efforts and disinclined to help our situation. She neglected housework, could neither sew nor cook, and didn't much want to learn. Essentially she lacked drive, the very quality for which I thought I had chosen her.

I found a third-floor walk-up apartment that I could afford in a rambling firetrap across the street from the Winchester Repeating Arms factory. Installed there under the eaves, we had a good view of the factory's parking lot and a sense of privacy that was entirely illusory since we had no front door. Our apartment and the apartment downstairs were on the same electric fuse, and if the couple downstairs plugged in their electric frying pan at the same time that we were using our toaster, all the lights went out. The only way to change the fuse was to get the basement key from the landlady, who lived in a different part of the city. Similarly, the water pressure could serve either our apartment or the one downstairs, but not both simultaneously. Whenever I was in the midst of a shower and well covered with soap, the woman downstairs would begin to draw a bath, shutting off our water entirely and leaving me shivering in the cold.

In search of a paradise where we could raise a family and lead the good life, I left the *Register* and took my bride to Cape Cod, where I found a job on a semiweekly. The natives were a clannish bunch, however, who kept us at arm's length socially and cheated us unconscionably in commercial transactions. I quit after four weeks.

We sought refuge with my mother in the white clapboard house and entered into what we thereafter and unoriginally called "the winter of our discontent." The economy was in a slump, and newspaper jobs were almost unobtainable. Each morning I would drive my wife to spend the day with her mother because she couldn't stand to stay with mine. Then I would set forth on my rounds, from one wretched little daily or weekly to another, my Volkswagen fishtailing demonically through the slush and snow. I met only failure and rejection. So we went to New York and took an efficiency in a flea-bitten hotel on Manhattan's West Side, on Eighty-sixth Street, directly across from what had been my maternal grandmother's house, where as a child I had spent Christmas week, cosseted by servants and spoiled by my aunt. Now, instead of having a chauffeur to drive me down to Times Square to see the lights, I made the rounds of employment agencies by subway and on foot. I put an ad in the *New York Times* but got no answers—not one. Defeated, we returned to my mother, and the winter snows piled deeper against the white clapboard house.

As my spirits sank, my wife's temper grew more frayed, her tongue sharper. We would huddle in our bedroom, keeping our voices low so that my mother would not over-hear us, and I would defend myself desperately against her accusations of failure. It was a difficult cause to plead be-cause I knew I was failing. At this worst possible time, she wanted to become pregnant, and she attributed to me her inability to do so. (Later, a gynecologist performed some minor cauterization on her and she became pregnant within a month.)

She stood in awe of my family, and my mother, who had never liked her, was awkward and ultimately unsuccessful in putting her at ease. While relying on my strength to shield her from hardship, she discovered my weakness and fallibil-ity, and passed up few opportunities to express her disap-pointment in me.

After ten weeks of this ordeal, the *Chicago Daily News* offered me a trial on the copy desk. I had never thought to live so far from New England, and I wouldn't have consid-ered it then if I had had any alternative. On two days' no-tice, we hurried to La Guardia Airport and took a plane to Chicago. As we sat side by side, waiting to take off, we turned to each other wordlessly and began to cry.

When we arrived, Chicago was experiencing a singularly bitter January, the skies remained a sullen gray, and the ice lay an inch thick on the sidewalks, as brittle and hard as glass. To conserve our money, we took a room in a YMCA hotel with one forty-watt bulb and a communal bath down the corridor. We both had colds, but as we gazed out the streaked window of our eighth-floor cell, looking down at the ice and the blinking colored lights of the girlie bar on the corner, our noses running, we were thinking in wonder, I like it. We felt a surge of hope borne aloft on the arctic wind. If we had not totally destroyed our regard for each other, we might yet build a life together. At least we had escaped from the white clapboard house, and I had the promise of a job. I have never been without one since, though the issue has sometimes been in doubt.

Eventually we accumulated the comforts to which we felt entitled: a little flat, called a "penthouse" because it was carved out of the attic space atop an ancient apartment building, furniture from Marshall Field's, concert and ballet tickets, and finally a son, whom we named after me. He weighed seven pounds, seven ounces, had the red face and bowed legs typical of the newborn, and screamed louder than any other baby in the hospital nursery. We were enormously pleased with him.

In the city room of the *Daily News* I advanced slowly, becoming in turn a slot man (the editor who runs the entire copy desk), a makeup editor, wire editor, and cable editor. We moved to a larger apartment, and when my wife became pregnant again, I bought a town house near the University of Chicago. In time, we had three children—a son and two daughters—to fill the house.

I lived with them there through eight awful years of undisciplined children, unmade beds, and unkempt rooms. Occasionally I hired contractors to wash or paint the walls or refinish the floors, or I would go to Field's and choose fabric for new slipcovers, but otherwise little was done to make the house more habitable. Children's books, incomplete puzzles, wooden blocks, dirty glasses, dismembered dolls, capsized kiddy cars, scraps of colored construction paper, potato chip crumbs, and unclad phonograph records were scattered everywhere. If I suggested that my wife clean house more vigorously, she resented my criticism. If I cleaned it myself, she resented the implied criticism. My only option was to endure the situation and shut up about it. My silence became my defense, but like everything else about me, she seemed to resent that too.

The condition of the house I could abide, but I choked on her spoiling the children. Seldom were they told to clean their rooms, make their beds, pick up their toys, hang up their clothes, or wash the dishes. But they were well-intentioned children and brighter than average. They could have learned.

My son had an inspired talent for the English language that he displayed from his earliest years. One bitter winter night when he was six, I took him to the hospital. Burning with fever and nearly dead from pneumonia in both lungs, he slumped against me in the taxi, gasping asthmatically, his little bony hand holding mine. I carried him into the emergency room, and there, as the doctors examined him, he began to show off by identifying medical instruments. I could have murdered him. When he named and correctly pronounced the sphygmomanometer, the device that measures blood pressure, the resident was so impressed that he called his colleagues to hear my son perform. They sat him on the edge of the examining table, his eyes glassy with fever, his emaciated rib cage heaving at every breath, and made him do verbal stunts.

"Dammit!" I roared. "My son is supposed to be in oxygen."

He stayed in an oxygen tent for several days. Into the back of his right hand ran an intravenous needle, the first that I had ever seen, though I have seen many since. The I.V. infiltrated often, and the needle had to be moved to new sites. The nurses could do that skillfully, but the residents and interns needed practice in order to run the needle into my son's tiny veins. They jabbed and jabbed, probing deeply but missing the vein, persisting in their attempts for five and ten minutes at a time while my son wept and struggled against the pain. "Please! PLEASE! *PLEASE!*" he wailed. He had been taught that he could have what he wanted if he said please, but that no longer worked.

My son grew strong in time, two inches taller than I and twenty pounds heavier, a horror when crossed but otherwise exhibiting angelic charm and wit. At twelve he was reading Dante for pleasure, along with monster comic magazines. Girls found him irresistible. So did I. (I never see him now.)

My daughters were slightly less articulate than my son but infinitely better behaved, as little girls usually are. Until I became a parent, I assumed that sex-typed behavior is acquired, but my own children convinced me that it arises spontaneously. Certainly I did not teach manliness to my son; he simply exuded it from infancy. Similarly my daughters acquired femaleness from within themselves. I marveled at their innate femininity, their grace, the delicacy of their play. But though I thought I understood them very well, I felt clumsy and oafish with them, as if I had been dressed in a gorilla suit and sent to play among the elves. Later, both before and after my transfiguration, one of my daughters, alone among my three children, tried to make friends with me, made presents for me, came to visit me at the office. But she could not overcome my awkwardness. My son remained a mystery to me until the day we parted.

Postsurgical transsexuals often marry and adopt children. One prevalent view holds that these adopted children serve a cosmetic purpose, like the toy poodles carried about by some women, but I believe I might have become a passable mother. Like any normal woman, I find myself beguiled by other people's children. I smile inanely at them and long to cuddle them. I would like to have done that with my own children, but I always thought such conduct inappropriate in a father. I approached the duties of fatherhood with heavy deliberation if slight aptitude. Because I considered my wife overindulgent toward the children, I played the stern disciplinarian. It was I who always said no to requests for extra money, candy, and staying up late to watch television, and she who always said yes. So the children learned to ask her first. She was the bountiful mother. I was the ogre.

We fought bitterly, stridently, constantly, and invariably I came off second-best. She had a spectacular talent for finding my vulnerable points. Often her attacks contained metaphysical hints at offenses so dark that she could not name them and would most certainly never forgive them. Her recriminations enveloped me like a black fog, impenetrable, blinding, yet insubstantial. I could not defend myself because I could not grasp the accusations. I don't know how she did it.

But if I could not understand my wife's animosity, I speculated about it a good deal and was prepared to concede that she must have had her reasons. Eventually, after I had come to understand myself better, I even evolved a theory to fit the circumstances: I concluded, however ironically in the light of my own hidden feelings, that she was afraid of men. She had told me that her father, described as an irresponsible, hard-drinking Irishman, had deserted his family when she was an infant. Alone and unaided, her mother had raised her and an older sister, and in addition had had her own mother to support. I pictured these four women huddled at the kitchen table—the grandmother, the mother, and the two little girls—banded together in female solidarity against a hostile male world. Callers were discouraged. But having married me, there was now a man she could not exclude from her life, a man she must even allow into her bed. She saw in me those male attributes she had come to hate and fear, accentuated all the more by my determination to practice them and be as much of a man as I could. And to the extent that I succeeded in those efforts, I failed in my marriage. She detested what I was—almost as much as I did.

Sometimes she went at me by direct, frontal assault.

"You're fat!" she spat at me one night.

I realized with horror that she was right. I retreated to the bathroom and inspected myself in the mirror. I was grotesque. My trouser waist size had expanded from thirty-two inches to thirty-six. My mustache made me look like a walrus. My chest and belly were matted with hair, while the bristles on my head were receding. My jowls wobbled. I was filled with disgust and loathing. As I lay on my back in bed, I saw that hairy belly rising before me like a hideous growth, imprisoning me ever more deeply in the ugliness of manhood. I was trapped, buried alive.

I began to diet and also to seek avenues of escape. I rejoined the Episcopal church choir in which we both had once sung. I wormed my way into the sailboat-racing fraternity, sometimes crewing in the smaller one-designs but more often in the big offshore boats, most of them forty feet or longer overall, on whose sails the wind exerted terrifying forces. In fair weather, they created an impression of great speed, though in fact they seldom recorded more than twelve knots. But when the wind piped and the waves built, the boats thrashed and lurched in an alarming manner. And if a gale caught us with everything standing, my heart filled with cold fear. But though I was often frightened, I continued to sail. It was a man's world, women at that time being almost uniformly excluded. If I could survive there, I could prove myself a man. In my third season I joined a boat that cruised more often than it raced, and I volunteered to do the cooking. I coveted the role of housekeeper, doing the marketing before each cruise and catering to the wishes of the men. Unfortunately, I was one of the few aboard who could handle the headsails on the narrow, pitching foredeck. So while the owner's wife stayed below as cook, I remained on deck, drenched and terrified in the stiff winds, sometimes having to claw at the acres of rebellious nylon until the blood ran from beneath my fingernails.

Sailing presented only one of my escapes. After four years as a copy editor on the *New Haven Register* and five more on the *Chicago Daily News,* I had moved over to the *Chicago Tribune,* where I shortly became a feature writer on the *Tribune Sunday Magazine.* It was a lovely job, and I reveled in it for ten years. I had become a journalist out of a passion for writing, but for the nine previous years I had been restricted to repairing the crippled prose of others. Now I could write, and not merely routine news stories either, but full-blown magazine features with long, rococo descriptive passages and gothic towers of emotion. Where most reporters were limited to two or three pages of copy for a story, I was given liberty to write twenty or thirty if the fancy took me. And it did. I grew famous, my name blazoned on the sides of the circulation trucks and broadcast on radio and television promotions. I was considered an immediate expert on every subject I covered and was invited to appear on television panels and address women's clubs. Sales clerks recognized my name and supermarket checkers knew my face. I was hired to teach at Northwestern University's journalism school and asked to lecture to convocations of editors. It was heavenly.

Sometimes I wrote medical stories for which I spent days

and weeks in the hospital, dressed in operating-room greens, absorbing the atmosphere until the surgeons would joke about my becoming board-certified and the patients would seize my hand in the corridors and say, "I want to thank you for everything you've done for me, doctor."

I specialized in the most masculine stories I could find or devise, anything that would take me into a world where I could study and enjoy the way men conduct themselves— for even though I differed from them, I liked their company. I wrote about Army helicopter pilots, firemen, high-tension linemen, parachute jumpers, treasure divers, game wardens, Great Lakes ore boat sailors. I slept in the open with the Green Berets while snow fell on my face. I learned scuba diving and descended to Spanish wrecks on the ocean floor. I clung to the sides of fire engines hurtling through the Chicago streets on winter nights. I spent countless nights with policemen, breaking through doors on vice raids and accompanying them into the most perilous cesspools of the city where snipers would fire on us from the windows of public-housing high rises.

In the office, these stories came to be known as my series about "the danger men," and by implication, I became a man who lived on familiar terms with danger, an artist at the typewriter but a lion in the streets. Curiously, I was seldom afraid, though I could claim no credit for that. I would stay close to my protectors—the beat cops or the company commander or the chief diver—and put my trust wholly in their hands. I enjoyed this position of dependence, though at the time I believed my pleasure rose from fraternizing with men of courage. Some of this courage rubbed off on me by association, and in the office I was met by ranks of respectful eyes.

From these exploits I would return to the bosom of my

family to be reviled as a tyrant and a sadist. No prize won, no achievement honored, was to be considered in my defense. If my wife knew that I was one of Chicago's most eminent journalists, she exhibited neither pleasure nor pride in the knowledge. I might be a hero at the paper, but at home I was barely to be tolerated. Increasingly my life centered on the office; home became merely where I slept and changed my clothes.

Then Maria entered my office world. I have fallen in love with many women during my life as a man, but only two did I love with all my heart. One I loved rationally and completely, but Maria I loved passionately, insanely, obsessively. She had the lush, ripe fullness characteristic of many Italian girls. Her hair fell in soft bangs that almost concealed huge, long-lashed eyes. Her moods—first solemn, then spectral, then inanely giddy—changed faster than ripples on water. She thought I was the greatest writer since Dante, and parched as I was for approval, I drank in her praise.

When Maria first came to work at the *Tribune,* I took no notice of her—or as little notice as possible, considering her legs, which were generously revealed by the miniskirts in fashion that year. At first I never thought to pursue a torrid affair with an editorial employee seventeen years younger than I. I had been a virgin when I married at the age of twenty-nine, and in the succeeding years I had remained technically faithful to my wife.

A few blocks east of Tribune Tower there is a park with fountains and terrazzo walks and fenced terrazzo platforms cantilevered out over the water. Here I took Maria for a noontime walk. We stood on one of the platforms like passengers on a cruise ship, looking down into the water and talking softly. As if on cue, we turned toward each other, knowing quite well what was about to happen, and kissed. I thought then that she looked unspeakably sad. On the way back to the tower, she made me release her hand. "I don't want to see you outside of the office anymore," she said.

But I could no more have stopped pursuing her than I could have stopped breathing. I had thought myself old, and she made me young; I had thought my emotions frozen, and she had melted them; I had resigned myself to death, and she had awakened me. But what a tormented awakening! I was demonic. I brought her gifts of books and laid them reverently on her desk as on an altar. I drove past her apartment building at night in hopes of catching a glimpse of her. I telephoned her in the evening and talked for hours. When I took my wife and children on vacation to an island in Penobscot Bay, I spent the summer afternoons writing long letters to her. I wrote her poems.

I wish that we were married,
I wish that we could dwell
In an air-conditioned townhouse with a hi-fi and
   a television and disposal and machinery that
   rids
The atmosphere of moisture and a whole bunch of
   kids.

I wish that I were younger,
I wish that I were rich
And cool enough to con you with a copper-plated
   pitch
About your keen intelligence, your beauty, and
   your charms
Until you swooned from flattery and tumbled in
   my arms.

I wish that it were morning,
I wish that I'd awake
And find you here beside me, so near that I could
  take
You in my arms and love you until we shook the
  bed.
I wish that you adored me.
I wish that I were dead.

My thoughts had in fact taken on a suicidal hue. The nightly quarrels at home left me crippled with pain. My every remark was used against me. One night at dinner I tried to steer the conversation toward Mary McCarthy's *The Group*, which I had read because my wife had enjoyed it. I thought at least we might talk about a novel without rancor. I mentioned one of the characters in the book who had behaved with particular dishonor and commented on the skill with which her odious characteristics had been revealed.

"She's just like you," my wife retorted, the familiar fury blazing up in her eyes, her mouth twisting into that tight little smile that always marked a blow well landed, a cut deftly inflicted. The old sense of horror squeezed my stomach with a cold hand, and I counterattacked. I don't remember what I said, but it sufficed to fuel another blazing row.

These arguments usually erupted at the dinner table in the presence of the children and invariably shifted to my wife's determination to divorce me. She knew that I abhorred fights in front of the children and that, as a strictly reared Episcopalian, I would not consider divorce. But no words or action of mine could quench the fires of her rage, nor could I understand how I had offended her and earned this searing resentment. Night after night in the darkness of our bedroom, I pleaded for mercy, and night after night she informed me with grim satisfaction that she could never forgive my nameless crimes.

In the office, my agony grew both worse and sweeter. Maria steadfastly spurned my attentions, yet she was not so foolish as to deny the magnetic flux that surged between us. Each time our eyes met across the room, we acknowledged the ruinous sway we held over each other, though neither of us understood its nature. I'm sure she supposed that I wanted to penetrate her, and indeed I did, though what I wanted was to blend my body with hers, to stand inside that lovely frame and feel the world through her senses, to gaze at my mirror reflection from her dark eyes and know myself as a woman. The impossibility of this obsession drove me to despair, and in despair at last I sought a reckless relief.

The Vietnam War appeared to offer a likely and easy vehicle for self-destruction. Like many *Tribune* writers, I had repeatedly asked to be sent to Vietnam and had as often been refused. Now under the influence of too many lunchtime cocktails, I ambushed Clayton Kirkpatrick, the *Tribune*'s editor, in the corridor outside his office, and made a final and impassioned plea. Despite his known antipathy to drunks on the editorial payroll, he took pity on me and said that I could go. I felt very much the tragic hero.

My sense of the dramatic informed me that, properly staged, my final evening with Maria could scale the heights of pathos. She cooked dinner in her apartment, which I had so often passed in my loony nocturnal rounds, and as a farewell gift I presented her with a phonograph and a recording of Chopin's First Piano Concerto, whose melancholy insistence I thought suited the mood I was trying to establish. We lay on the living room floor, listened to Chopin, and talked. When the hour grew late and I had not gone home, her defenses weakened, and she lay down with me on her bed and permitted me to make love to her.

The Vietnam War was at its height in the fall of 1968 when I arrived in Saigon. I took a cheap room in a hotel at the end of an alley and from there I would go forth to the battlefield once or twice a week. The military made it absurdly easy by maintaining what amounted to a scheduled helicopter service from Saigon to every battle area in Indochina. A correspondent could ride free merely by presenting his press credentials.

Those were eerie flights. To hasten debarkation during landings under fire, the doors and seat belts had been removed from the helicopters. I would sit in the doorway with the toe of my boot sticking out into the slipstream and watch the landscape pass below. Sometimes we followed a river, its banks chemically stripped of foliage to deny concealment to the enemy. Or we might cut straight across a "triple canopy" jungle, so called because the foliage grew at three distinct levels and consequently required three applications of defoliating chemical before it was entirely destroyed. The motto of the military crews that specialized in this work was "Only we can prevent a forest."

Before I could go on a combat operation, I usually had to check in at division headquarters, where a bird colonel would brief me for my private enlightenment, giving me the broad, strategic picture. I remembered my days as a buck sergeant when I was forced to show extreme deference to such full colonels who were now offering me coffee and respectfully answering my questions. As a correspondent, the Army told me, I held the "simulated rank" of major. The briefings seldom varied. The colonel stood with a pointer before an array of maps on which lines and arrows had been drawn to represent ourselves and the enemy. Captured Communist weapons, always including a mortar tube and a Russian AK-47 automatic rifle, would be displayed on the walls. Never having cared much for either bird colonels or broad, strategic pictures, I lost no time in getting out of those places.

My consuming interest lay in combat itself and those who endured it, the rifle companies composed of perhaps a hundred bedraggled men, commanded by a captain and living in a shell-torn hooch or out in the open. They were very young, the enlisted men seldom more than nineteen years old and the officers in their mid-twenties. They were often exceedingly dirty and suffering from jungle rot, which spread in the most appalling rashes up their thighs and over their crotches.

But they were the most hospitable souls on earth. Because they were young and I was forty-one, because I was the first newspaper reporter most of them had ever seen in combat, because they thought that they were tough and I was not, they shielded me with touching gallantry. They dug my foxhole for me and offered me my choice of the tastiest C rations, which they had hoarded in their packs. Once when we were surrounded and so heavily under fire that the resupply choppers could not reach us, they offered me the last drops of water in their canteens, a gesture of charity that finds no parallel in civilian life. If I elected to accompany one patrol, three or four others would volunteer to go along, not because it was their turn but because they thought they should be on hand to keep me out of trouble.

I was not as helpless as they supposed. To my surprise, I remembered the infantry training I had received twenty-three years before: how to form a skirmish line, how to seek shelter behind a rise in the ground, how to wash a pair of socks in my helmet. I learned how to fire and field-strip an M-16 rifle and, whenever I could, would pick one off the battlefield. The Geneva Convention disapproves of armed correspondents, who may be executed as spies if captured, but the enemy was trying to kill me in any event, and it satisfied my sense of fair play when I was able to shoot back.

Often I was not. "I feel sort of naked out here without a weapon," I remarked to a company commander one afternoon as we advanced in a skirmish line toward an unseen enemy force. We were at the center of the line, about six feet apart.

"Why the hell did you come out here without a weapon?" he retorted heatedly. Diplomatic niceties aside, I wasn't the slightest use to him unarmed.

I had gone out there for several reasons, the same ones that had impelled me to write about "the danger men": curiosity about the nature of manhood, reckless contempt for my own skin, perverse pleasure in the frailties that set me apart from my heroes, and the occasional twinge of pride when I managed to equal them in strength or daring, when I truly felt myself a part of male society.

In this last respect I was handicapped by the flaws in my male façade, particularly by my inability to void my bladder in the presence of other men. God, the agonies I have suffered from that affliction! One day I flew from dawn until noon jammed into a battalion command helicopter and wishing with increasing fervor that I could go to the bathroom. I cared not at all that I had a splendid view of the battle. With his radio, the battalion commander could move his men about the Mekong River paddies beneath us like pieces on a chessboard, and we could see them jump on his order—men scuttling across a field to shelter in a treeline, or a column of tanks advancing up a road, or three rounds from a 105-mm. howitzer demolishing a troublesome village.

At noon we landed to refuel the chopper and eat a C-ration lunch. I skulked off behind some bushes and was just about to find heavenly release when the colonel clumped up in his jungle boots, his pistol on his hip, a convivial smile smeared across his face, to join me in communal urination. I could have killed him. I had to go into combat with a rifle company two hours later just to find a little privacy and salvage what remained of my kidneys.

From these sorties I would return to my hotel room in Saigon. I would shower and change into civilian clothes and check the mail for a letter from Maria, but none ever came in the two months I was in Vietnam. Then I would go to the officers club in the Rex Hotel for drinks and a steak. Later, as night fell over Saigon, I would sit on the roof of the Rex with more drinks and watch the motor-scooter traffic swirl around the fountain below while over the outskirts of the city the parachute flares burned and the tracers cut bright dotted lines across the black sky.

The next morning I would settle at my typewriter, and the copy would gush from a well of emotion, twenty and thirty pages in a single day. I had never seen and heard and smelled so clearly, never written so easily. I was infatuated with Vietnam, where the rivers teemed with fish, the trees hung heavy with fruit, and the ground nurtured exotic vegetables, growing wild where they were not cultivated. I thought I had never seen a place so beautiful. These people could live like kings if only they would stop killing each other.

But I myself was not killed or even scratched. Once while

flying combat assaults with the First Air Cavalry, my helicopter took a round in the vertical stabilizer, but so slight was the damage that we didn't discover it until we returned to base for lunch.

Still, it's a wonder any of us survived that day. In seventeen hours of flying, we made fourteen combat assaults, taking fire on almost every one. In fairness, it should be stipulated that we gave as good as we got. Before each assault, the landing zone would be prepped with artillery fire, a barrage that often lasted all night. Then as we plummeted down over the rim of the jungle clearing, our two door-gunners would open a deafening clatter of machine-gun fire, the bullets slashing the fronds from the trees. Nor did we linger on the ground but disgorged our load of riflemen as fast as we could, shoving and kicking any who seemed reluctant to go. Freed of their weight, we took off at once, just clearing the treetops on the opposite rim, striving for speed in preference to altitude because this was the "killing zone," the place of greatest danger from the enemy, and they loved to shoot down a helicopter when they could.

That night they got one. We were flying our last trip of the day, dropping flares to illuminate a resupply mission at a landing zone that was under heavy fire. (We had "inserted" a rifle company there that morning, and they were in deep trouble.) Below us we could see one of our sister choppers taking off by flarelight. It charged across the clearing, rose to surmount the jungle rim, and was caught in three converging streams of AK-47 fire. We could see the tracers smashing into it, see the aircraft falter, then fall backward, its rotor blades slashing the trees, and crash tailfirst in the jungle.

Miraculously, the four crewmen survived, though two

were injured. I talked with them the next morning after a medevac chopper had brought them out. But I was beginning to lose my taste for combat. It is difficult enough to go into battle under the duress of discipline and orders. It was harder still for me to go there on my own volition, to seek out a firefight and place myself in the midst of it. Each night before I set out on an operation, I lay awake in my hotel room, my heart pounding with fright, and contemplated the law of averages. I had come under fire four times . . . six times . . . eight times, and had emerged whole. Would I survive the tenth confrontation? And the twelfth? My nerve was failing, and I knew I had to leave.

And so one December morning, I was driven out to the air base by two sergeants who had tipped me off to many fights and had an exaggerated respect for my courage, never suspecting how thinly it was stretched. The terminal was a cattle pen of humanity, milling apprehensively beneath the sullen gaze of armed and uniformed Vietnamese. I was suffocating in the fear and crowdedness of the place when an exotic Oriental girl in a Pan Am uniform found me in the throng at the ticket counter. "Mr. Hunt? Mr. Hunt? May I have your passport, please?" She guided me through the crowd, seated me in solitary splendor in a Pan Am station wagon, and had me driven across the field to a waiting jet. As I climbed the ramp and saw the scrubbed American faces of the stewardesses, I felt as if I were already home in my own country.

I allowed them to stow my combat pack with my jungle boots strapped on the outside, and settled gratefully into my seat. The other passengers at last arrived by bus and boarded. The door swung shut. The engines started. I put on a pair of headphones and turned the selector to the airplane's classical music channel. Of all the civilities that I had missed in Vietnam, I had yearned most for classical music. Now the airplane was lifting, starting a steep climb-out because even here, on the outskirts of Saigon, the enemy sometimes fired on commercial airliners—and occasionally hit them. The music system was playing the largo movement from Dvořák's *New World* Symphony, the melody called "Going Home." I stared down at the Mekong River Delta passing beneath our wings, at the winding waterways and the rice paddies and the jungle where I had gone so often and where good friends were fighting even now as I staged my retreat. The roar of the engines and the deeply orchestrated chords of the music shook me with anguish and beauty. I pressed my face against the window so that nobody would see me and wept uncontrollably.

No one met me at the airport in Chicago. I took a taxi, not to my house but to Maria's apartment. It was after midnight when I got there. She was white-faced and withdrawn. She had quit her job at the *Tribune* to escape me, she said. It was the best job she had ever had, she told me, but I had forced her to give it up. I was not to telephone or write her or make any attempt to see her. She laid down her restrictions one by one like a judge pronouncing sentence.

Numb with fatigue and grief, I unpacked the presents I had brought her: four cartons of PX cigarettes; a comb, carved from some strange Asian wood; a pair of jade earrings that I had had made for her by a Saigon jeweler; and my tiny Olympia typewriter that I had bought to take to Vietnam and on which I had written so many pages of war correspondence and love letters.

At two o'clock in the morning I could no longer postpone my departure. Maria called a taxi for me, and I left.

SIX

Many people have nightmares after combat, but mine were trying only in their monotony. I would dream that I was marching down a red dirt road lined on one side with barbed-wire entanglements. Tanks and trucks and scrawny Vietnamese troops in camouflage uniforms passed in endless procession. The Vietnamese smiled at me evilly, calling out in their harsh language and beckoning me to turn around and follow them, but I plodded on in the opposite direction. Some nights I marched like that for what seemed hours and awoke in the morning exhausted.

The waking was the bad part. It brought me back to a life that seemed to lie in fragments at my feet. Maria had gone. That was the first thought of the morning, and it shocked me into full consciousness. I had gone to war to prove my vigor and my manhood, and she hadn't been impressed at all.

Neither had my wife. She viewed my Vietnam experience as a sort of Rotary Club excursion that I had taken merely to entertain myself and evade my responsibilities to her. If it was war I wanted, well, she could give me plenty of that at my own dinner table. I hadn't been home two days before she resumed full-battery fire about divorcing me. With the children, as before, stationed as forward observers. One night when I was doing the supper dishes, her rage reached such a peak that she grabbed the telephone book and began furiously to hunt for the home number of the lawyer who had drawn my will. "I'm not going to put up with this anymore," she stormed, again failing to specify what "this" was. "I'm going to call Reuben."

"Go ahead," I replied, secure in the knowledge that Reuben had an unlisted number. "No, on second thought, you leave Reuben alone. He's my lawyer, not yours. If you're going to mess around with divorce, get one of the Rinellas. They're supposed to be the best divorce lawyers in town."

She flung the telephone book down furiously, momentarily defeated. But she was a wily antagonist. A few minutes later I heard her upstairs, giving one of my daughters a bedtime bath. "Daddy's a liar!" she said, her voice raised to reach me in the living room. "Daddy lies all the time."

I could not combat it. Already I had forfeited the children's love. She gave them junk food and cheap plastic toys while I offered nothing but prohibitions. I could not bring myself to compete in the purchase of potato chips and Silly Putty. I had lost them. I had lost Maria. And I was fast losing myself.

The drumfire of divorce threats was battering me to pieces. She had even enlisted her best friend, Ellen, to testify against me in court. (Under Illinois law, a plaintiff in an uncontested divorce is required to appear in court with two witnesses. Usually well rehearsed in the ritual testimony— "Did he treat her in a cold, cruel, and contemptuous manner?" "Was her health adversely affected so that she had to seek the services of a physician?"—they can answer with impunity.) I liked Ellen, and it hurt that she had agreed to testify against me. In any event, I had no stomach for courtroom fights.

A few days later, my wife told me that she had made an appointment to see Bernie Rinella.

"Good!" I snapped.

And a few evenings after that, when I was down at the playground supervising the children on the jungle gym, she joined me looking unwontedly chastened. "What will you do if I don't keep my appointment with Mr. Rinella?" she asked.

"Then, my dear, I will sue *you* for divorce."

I was as astonished as she, for I knew I meant it. I could not save her. I could not save the children. But I could damned well save myself. I had no idea what sort of life I might salvage out of this wreckage, but if I had learned anything in Vietnam, it was that I did not want to die.

Divorce was a slow and tedious business in Illinois in those days, and the grounds were limited. Uncontested cases like ours were usually based on charges of mental cruelty, which were easy enough to adjudicate, but the judges wouldn't process these suits until they were assured that equitable property settlements had been worked out, and such arrangements might take months or even years. In our case the lawyers haggled happily (they were fraternity brothers) and endlessly over alimony and insurance and taxes, though I was willing to pay well for my freedom. I did pay then, and still do now.

We continued to live in the same house, putting the children to bed each night in our ritual way. One of us would

CARL A. RUDISILL LIBRARY
LENOIR RHYNE COLLEGE

grab the hands and the other the feet, and we would swing the victim like a sack of potatoes, three times in ever-increasing arcs, chanting: "Then we take her . . . and throw her . . . throw her . . . THROW her . . . A-WAAY!" On the last word, the victim would be semihurled into bed, giggling wildly.

We continued to have Ellen over for supper. Even though she had promised to testify against me, I bore her no ill will and still drove her home at the end of the evening. She had been a freshman at the University of Chicago when she had first come to us as a baby-sitter, and now she was a graduate student in Scandinavian languages with a master's degree already in hand and working for her doctorate. She was my wife's closest confidante.

One night as I was driving her home, I suggested that we stop off somewhere and have a drink.

"I'd like to," she said.

We had several drinks and finished the night in bed in a motel.

It was the end of March, the birth of spring, and the beginning of the happiest seven years I would ever know as a man. We made love constantly and everywhere—in motels, in state parks, in friends' houses, in Ellen's apartment when her roommate was absent. Ellen had to teach me everything. Though I had been married for thirteen years and had sired three children, I knew almost nothing about sex. Ellen, twenty years younger than I, knew a great deal.

On long walks in the woods or lying in the grass, we talked about how we would be married after my divorce. Sometimes, resting silently in bed, tired from our lovemaking, we would look at each other with dreamy, satisfied smiles, as if we had done something terribly clever. Ellen was not pretty by conventional standards—her face was too square, her nose too broad, her figure too ample—but her expression was stamped with decency and an open honesty that I loved. I thought it was the nicest face I had ever seen. I think so still, though I have not seen it for many months.

My wife did not ask me where I was going when I rose from the dinner table each night and left the house without a word of explanation or farewell. No matter what transgressions she ascribed to me, she retained absolute trust in my fidelity. Each night I would go to Ellen, and usually we would drive down to the Thunderbird Motel, where I would register us under an assumed name.

The sweetness of our ardor was heightened by the knowledge that it was to be short-lived. In just four weeks, Ellen would leave for six months' study in Norway. We made the most of the time we had, ending with a three-day trip into Indiana, where we stayed at a state park lodge. Spring was well advanced there, the buds already bursting. We chased each other through the woods and scrambled from rock to rock along the river. Then we lay in the sun amid the spring flowers while Ellen read aloud to me from Dorothy Sayers's *Gaudy Night*. I had never been so happy.

Ellen had not been in Norway long when she wrote to say that she wouldn't marry me after all. It was characteristic of her, I was to discover, that she could love me while we were together and tire of me when we were apart. I arranged to take a week off from work and bought an airplane ticket to Oslo, prepared to fight for the happiness that had been granted me, but Ellen called shortly before I was to leave and urgently asked me not to come to her. Reluctantly I accepted her wishes, concluding bitterly that I should have known God would not allow me such joy.

Ellen's defection obliged me to confront another uncomfortable truth: If I had been prepared to leave my legal wife and children in the expectation of living with Ellen, then surely I must summon the resolution to leave them with no expectations at all.

I found a one-room furnished apartment and paid a month's rent in advance. That night at dinner, I told my wife and children, "I'm going away again tomorrow." The word *again* was calculated. The children were accustomed to my going away on assignments for the *Tribune,* and I wanted them to associate this departure with those others that had not upset their lives. I wanted to make this upheaval as easy on them as possible, though I had no reason to suppose that they would be unduly bothered if they never saw me again. "But this time," I continued, "I'll be staying right here in Chicago so that I can still come and take you out to play."

My wife saw what I was up to and was not about to be topped. Instantly and without a word, she rose from her chair and, leaving her supper unfinished, stalked from the house. A few minutes later she reappeared with June Gibbs, a next-door neighbor. June looked at me with revulsion, as if I had just been exposed as a child-molester.

"Come on and help me get your nightclothes, kids," my wife said. "We're going to sleep over at June's tonight."

Gathering up slippers and teddy bears and toothbrushes, the children followed her solemnly out the front door, white-faced and scared. They knew something awful was happening now and that they would suffer for it. On the front doorstep, with the children gathered about her, my wife turned and fixed me with a sardonic smile. She had taken the last trick after all.

I spent the final night alone in my house, and the next morning I put my two suitcases and my old Smith-Corona typewriter in the back of my station wagon and drove off to begin a new life. Neither my wife nor my children came out of June's to say good-bye.

I had read a good deal about divorce by then. Books and friends alike had told me that leaving the familiar comforts of home was the worst of the ordeal. All day I waited for fears and doubts to assail me. It will come when I'm alone in my new apartment tonight, I told myself. I'll probably be a basket case.

The orange sunlight of a May evening was streaming through my tenth-floor windows as I let myself into my new home and locked the door behind me. I mixed myself a gin gimlet and lowered myself gratefully into an upholstered chair from which I could admire the view. Beyond the houses across the street, Lincoln Park lay green and bucolic, and beyond the park a single sailboat seemed motionless on Lake Michigan. I felt content.

That autumn Ellen returned to Chicago and called me. I happened to be entertaining another woman at dinner that evening, a woman to whom I had already made love once in an unrewarding way and, I supposed, would again. It was not a relationship from which I took much pleasure. Ellen, I suspected, was feeling lonely and let down after the stimulation of foreign study. We met the next day, and within three weeks she had moved into my one-room efficiency with me. We lived there all that winter, giving ourselves entirely to the delights of table and bed. Both of us gained weight alarmingly. I bought a television set so she could watch the Sunday football games. At night I made sandwiches, which we washed down with beer while watching British mystery films on television. In the morning I cooked vast breakfasts of pancakes and sausages, bacon and eggs, French toast and syrup. In between, we made love, and I tried to master the techniques of satisfying her lusty appetites, not always successfully.

"You're the worst man to go to bed with," she told me one morning, "and the best man to get up with."

At Christmas she received a card from my wife, forwarded by Ellen's parents in Massachusetts. Inside it my wife had written desperately, "Ellen, where are you?" We laughed at the irony, though I felt a twinge of Episcopalian conscience.

In February my divorce was granted. It might have happened sooner had my wife not dragged her feet. Despite all those years of threatening me with divorce, she had never believed that I would leave her. She had delayed in the expectation that I would come home to her, humbled and repentant. It took months for her lawyer and mine to convince her of the improbability of my return.

In March Ellen and I rented an apartment in the building across the street from our efficiency and set about furnishing it. To simplify such complexities as credit cards, life insurance, and mail delivery, we decided to get married. Neither of us had dared confess to our parents that we were living together, but when I wrote my mother of our plans, she smelled a rat, took the next plane, and arrived in Chicago unannounced to save me from "this disaster."

We did our best to reconcile her to our marriage. For the occasion of meeting my mother at dinner, Ellen bought a new dress, a green knit print with sailor collar and tie. She looked adorable, but my mother remained unmoved. She had been happy enough to see me divorced ("We none of us liked her from the beginning," she had written me), but she could not swallow this alliance with a girl of no social distinction and, worst of all, a girl twenty years my junior. It was absolutely disgusting. She got me alone the next day at luncheon and bullied and wheedled and wept, but I was forty-three years old, and Ellen had made me enough of a man to stand up to my mother for once.

Ellen's parents weren't crazy about the match either, but they nevertheless did us proud at the wedding. We were married in the little Massachusetts church that Ellen had attended as a child, and my mother drove up for the ceremony. Ellen's younger sister, in a garden-party dress and a broad-brimmed straw hat with ribbon streamers down the back, played a Liszt étude, and Ellen's father, an accomplished musician, played an oboe passage from the Bizet Symphony in C Major. Our vows were traditional.

A champagne reception followed on the blacktop driveway of Ellen's parents' house. Ellen looked beautiful in a green silk dress with gathered bodice that she had made herself. I wore a new summer-weight Brooks Brothers suit that Ellen had insisted I buy. The June sun beamed down on us, the trees were in full leaf, and the champagne had a pleasurable dryness. As I looked at Ellen smiling among the guests —so young and dear—I wished that we could freeze this moment and preserve it.

SEVEN

We had been married for eight months when I confessed to Ellen that abstractly I had always wanted to be a woman and specifically I wanted to wear a dress. I had never breathed this secret to a soul, and I wouldn't have told her now had we not learned to live together in perfect trust. The waves of sexuality that constantly broke over us, instead of securing me to my manhood, had torn me loose from my virile moorings. Ellen was so entirely woman—in body, dress, and behavior—that my love had become mixed with envy. I wanted to be like her. I knew that I had taken us to a dangerous turning, and my heart hammered as I waited to see what she would do with the confidence I had just placed in her hands.

"That shouldn't be hard to arrange," she said. "I've probably got a dress that will fit you." Nothing was hard for Ellen to arrange. She could fix the electric toaster, fill out our income tax, upholster a chair, paint a room, make a soufflé. If she didn't know an answer, she could bluff until she found it.

She took from the closet the green knit sailor dress she had worn to meet my mother, then dressed me in panties and bra, slip and hose, and a curly brunette wig bought on sale at the corner supermarket. I submitted passively, too inexperienced and too agitated to do up my own zipper. She led me into the bathroom and made up my face with eyebrow pencil and mascara, eyeliner and eye shadow, blusher and powder, and finally lipstick.

"Press your lips together like this."

I did.

"All right, now you can look."

I stared at myself in the bathroom mirror.

"Jesus! That mustache has got to go."

Without a word or moment of thought, I took my razor and shaved off my mustache. Later Ellen told me that this more than anything else had revealed to her the profound depth of my obsession. I had worn that mustache as long as she'd known me, and for many years before. That I should so casually obliterate it now appalled her.

For me it was a necessary and reflexive action. No woman outside of the circus wears a mustache, and I was seeing myself for the first time as a woman. And I could scarcely believe what the mirror revealed. For long minutes I stood in silent awe, inspecting my face from different angles. I moved in front of the full-length mirror on the front-hall closet.

"You're really quite attractive as a woman," Ellen pronounced judiciously.

The green knit accommodated itself adequately to my figure, setting off my hips, which had always been broad for a man. At the moment I was too bushy-browed and stubble-cheeked and heavy-jowled, but I was passable. I had seen lots of women far less presentable. And despite all the years of covering combat and police work, there was something feminine in that face. And something exultantly happy.

We celebrated with a drink before I reluctantly undressed for the night. And then we made love, wildly and passionately, with me on the bottom in one of Ellen's nightgowns, imagining that I was the woman. Married male transsexuals usually have this fantasy, and I was to retain it for the five remaining years that I would live as an anatomic man. If Ellen suspected my thoughts as we made love, she submerged her apprehensions in satisfaction that we had discovered a way to lend variety to what had become a thoroughly well-worn act.

A few months later, Ellen abandoned graduate school, partly because she was bored and disillusioned with academia, partly because to rise in her field she would have to accept a faculty appointment outside Chicago, and I had made it clear that I would never leave the *Tribune*. She had completed all the requirements for her doctorate and had only to finish her dissertation, then about one-third done. She was writing on the theme of disguise in ancient Norse and Icelandic sagas, a subject I had suggested because my fourth-grade teacher had read aloud to us the story of how the great god Thor, in order to recover his stolen hammer, had dressed himself as a bride. Ellen's parents and I wanted her to complete her thesis and get her Ph.D., but she stuck to her decision and dumped the whole wagonful of work— quantities of four-by-six index cards and hundreds of typewritten pages—into the trash on the back porch.

She took a clerical job in an import-export firm promoting overpriced kitchen gadgets on television. With her office just three blocks from Tribune Tower, we met every noon and walked down to the Loop to shop for me, giggling at our preposterous secret and enjoying each other's company like two sisters. Later she would find nothing funny or enjoyable about our twisted relationship, but at first—perhaps through an effort of will, perhaps from love—she found it stimulating.

My appetite for clothes and makeup was insatiable and my tastes impossibly girlish. I had missed out on a whole childhood of ribbons and lace, and I burned to make up for lost time. If I bought a white slip, I immediately wanted a blue one, and if I had two nightgowns, I wanted four. And all had to be exaggeratedly feminine—lace-trimmed, flower-printed.

Ellen made the actual purchases—ostensibly for an absent sister—while I played the role of uncomfortable male, dragged unwillingly into these bowers of femininity. Thus she had ultimate control over my acquisitions, and she used it to try to curb my extravagance in fashion and cash. But it was hard to prevail against my lunacy. Consider the case of my first wig. I had to wear a wig to complete the illusion, not only because of my crew cut but also because of my receding hairline. We found one on sale in the budget basement of Marshall Field's. A honey-blond model, it had bangs and shoulder-length tresses ending in a flip. On a teenager it would have looked darling, but it made my craggy face look like a hatchet blade nestled in cotton balls. Yet I insisted on buying it. I have it still in its original box, on which I wrote in red grease pencil: "Nancy, b. 3/18/71" the date I put on the green sailor dress and released my demon from its cage.

If I ever have a husband, I shall feel aggrieved if he begins to turn into a woman right before my eyes. No woman should have to put up with that. But if Ellen felt any reproach, she kept it hidden from me—at least in those first years of my emergence. The fact was, I had never felt so close to another human being, so loved and so loving. We had become a unity, cleaving to the same standards of intellect and morality, the same tastes, reacting with simultaneous emotions of rage or joy or laughter. We could predict each other's thoughts unerringly because they would be our own.

Misunderstandings seldom occurred. Our discussions concerned not the settlement of differences but the enjoyment of similarities. At dinner we would analyze our love for each other and attempt to explain its wonders. Even now, I puzzle over the depth of my love for her, the delight I took in the way she walked, my pride in her competence, my happiness whenever I saw her face. How I reveled in the strength she gave me and in the comfort she took from me.

These, of course, are the marks of any well-suited married couple. To them we added an extra dimension of closeness, a sisterly bond that heightened our heterosexual union. By giving expression to my compulsion, we were joined in a conspiracy against convention. We talked and giggled and plotted like two girls at a pajama party. I was intoxicated by the sweetness of it. It was outrageous, comical, beautiful, dangerous, exciting, and we shared it and savored it like two delirious misers.

I supplied the motivating force to this lunacy, and Ellen played to my needs, which were boundless. I had always wanted a pink party dress with puffed sleeves and a bow in the back. Ellen made one for me, a preposterously unbecoming garment, designed exactly to my specifications, with a gathered skirt and a pink ribbon around the waist. With the shoulder-length tresses of my honey-blond wig and my middle-aged, male face, I must have looked unspeakably silly in it. But I was also unutterably happy. Ellen also made me a cornflower-blue linen dress with white lace around the neckline and cuffs. She made me cotton print skirts. She made me a green, sleeveless dress with a broad, white collar that lay outside a matching bolero jacket. And as a special treat, she made me a duplicate of her own wedding dress. She spent an enormous amount of time at the sewing machine.

Because I admired her and wanted to be like her in every respect, I got her to teach me how to sew—not as well as she but well enough to enable me to work with her. I bought another sewing machine for myself, and we spent a hundred evenings together making clothes.

In those days we both believed I was simply a transvestite, a man who derives pleasure from dressing like a woman. And a more commonplace derangement than most people suspect. For the first year I remained under cover, dressing like a woman only when at home in the evening and on weekends. We avoided social engagements because they prevented my wearing the clothes in which I felt comfortable. Yet I chafed at the restriction of the house, even as Ellen chafed at the inhibitions on our social life. After all, we could hardly dine out with friends if I was forever mincing about the house in skirts. Ellen endured this with good grace. At least she preferred it to the alternative that I suggested: appearing in public with me in this astonishing condition.

By now Ellen had resigned from the import-export business and, at my urging, enrolled in nursing school. Nursing had always appealed to me as the most womanly profession possible, and since I was manifestly unsuited to do it myself, I proposed to send Ellen out to do it for me. We missed her wages. My alimony payments took an appallingly large part of my own salary, and her tuition, uniforms, and books heavily increased the burden. (Books for the first term of her freshman year cost almost ninety dollars.)

To help out, Ellen took a night job two evenings a week as a medical-records clerk at the hospital across the street. On those nights I would flounce about the apartment alone, twitching my fanny and primping in front of the mirror, bored and lonely and aggrieved. I wanted to shave my legs, but Ellen had forbidden it. I wanted to manicure my toenails and pierce my ears and wear mesh stockings, but Ellen had balked at every turn. Sullenly I worked at my embroidery and brooded upon injustice.

Finally one warm summer evening when Ellen was at work and I had had rather a lot to drink, I kicked over the restraints. Typical of a woman, I can remember every detail of what I wore that night: a blue cotton print skirt with two rows of eyelet lace ruffles and a gathered waist, a white blouse with short puffed sleeves and a stand-up ruffled collar, white sandals, and a short, blond wig. In this get-up I decided to sally forth to the corner and mail a letter.

Never in the police raids or helicopter combat assaults I had covered had my heart beat so wildly with fear and exhilaration. Hazards lay about me on every hand. I might meet the landlord on the stairs. (He had once told me that he detested homosexuals, and I was sure he would lump me with them.) The cops might catch me. (Many cops take a sadistic delight in beating up drag queens.) A mad rapist might assault me.

Clutching my letter and my keys, I sneaked out of the apartment. I met no one. The night air smelled sweet and fresh and exciting. Fifty yards away stood the mailbox, a distant buoy in a threatening sea. I set course toward it, head high, heels clicking, fanny twitching. Now there were people, but no one paid me the least attention. A police car drove by without slowing. A small dog sniffed at my nylon ankles and went on about its business. Two men passed, homosexuals immersed in their preoccupations (disgusting, I thought). I might as well have been invisible, for all the notice taken of my public debut. Vaguely disappointed, I dropped the letter in the slot, flounced home again, up the stairs—still no landlord about—and locked myself inside. Safe! I felt like a fighter pilot returned to base from a perilous mission.

When I told Ellen about it, she was very annoyed but resigned. She could recognize the inevitable when she saw it.

A few nights later, I persuaded Ellen to accompany me. "Just around the block," I pleaded. We passed the doorman of a nearby apartment building and were gallantly hailed: "Good evening, ladies." At last! Recognition as a woman. I felt as if I had been awarded a Congressional Medal. (This reaction is not uncommon among transsexuals. Jan Morris, under similar circumstances, wrote, "If they had touched me with an accolade of nobility, or clad me ceremonially in crimson, I could not have been more flattered.")

Far from satisfied, my ambition to enter the world grew manic. A few nights later, again while Ellen was at work, I went out to a neighborhood bar and ordered a Drambuie. I had begged Ellen to go to a bar with me, but she had feared that men would try to pick us up. I feared no such event—I longed for it. And now as I sat at the bar, nursing my liqueur, two men did in fact strike up a conversation with me. Men often feel compelled to make conversational advances to unescorted women, whatever the poverty of their imaginations. "Well, you look nice and cool today. . . ." "Say, you must be getting coffee for the whole news department. . . ." "That's a pretty big bag for a nice-looking lady like you to be carrying. . . ." They don't really expect to get to your virtue, but they figure it never hurts to try, and anyway it's a conditioned reflex.

I accepted a second Drambuie from the two men but declined their invitation to drive somewhere out into the suburbs, supposedly to go dancing. Even at that early stage, I knew something about the risks of my adopted gender.

After that drab encounter, I was all the more eager to try my wings again. Not a week had passed before I did, this time at a larger and tonier bar that offered a three-piece band. I ordered a beer, and before I had finished it a second materialized before me. "From the gentleman sitting down at the corner," the bartender whispered. I looked at the gentleman sitting down at the corner and smiled in gratitude. As if on signal, he arose, drink in hand, and came to sit beside me. He was a photoengraver, a large man about my own age and beginning to run to fat. But he was a man, and I had caught him.

"Would you like to dance?" he asked.

Now what should I do? All my life I had abhorred the male body, my own no less than those that had surrounded me in dormitories and barracks and gymnasiums. They were all hairy and knobby and bony, and they had that revolting protuberance dangling between their legs. Now here was a male body proposing to seize me in clammy embrace and waltz me about the floor while panting into my ear. And I wanted it to do just that, not out of sexual arousal, I suspect, but from an urge to establish one more proof of my femininity. But I didn't know how to dance as a woman. Years ago I had danced passably as a man, getting by on the strength of a strong lead and a sense of rhythm. How would I know how to follow? Where was I supposed to stick my

116

arms? What if he embraced me too ardently and knocked my wig askew?

"I'd love to," I answered.

There was a momentary awkwardness while I sorted out my arms, and then we were off across the floor with my left arm tightened convulsively around his neck while I concentrated desperately on keeping my feet from under his.

He stopped and looked down at me pityingly. "Suppose you let me lead," he said.

I had thought he was leading. Certainly I had been trying my best to follow. I nestled my cheek against him, closed my eyes, and devoted my attention to the work at hand. It was a lovely dance, but he did not ask me for another.

Other such triumphs followed, and all of them I reported to Ellen, asking her always to go with me the next time. Having failed in my appeals to sympathy, I finally succeeded by touching the nerve of jealousy. I was going out drinking and dancing, and she was not. I was savoring the joys of bars and men, and she was reading nursing textbooks and working as a medical-records clerk. No one could accept such inequality, least of all Ellen with her well-developed sense of fair play. She capitulated at last.

Chicago's nightclub district centers on Rush Street, a garish collection of overpriced restaurants, art movie houses, and porno shops frequented largely by tourists, prostitutes of various sexual orientations, and suburbanites in town for a fling. One of the most prosperous enterprises on Rush Street was a place called Alfie's—later converted into a gay bar, to my sorrow—and here Ellen and I achieved our greatest victories as a couple of girls on the make. In those days Alfie's offered drinks at twenty-five cents apiece to "unescorted ladies," a canny practice that attracted droves of single girls and in turn regiments of men. If a man picked up a girl and her tab, he was charged full price retroactively for all her drinks, thus recovering Alfie's investment in her. If the girl failed to attract a man, she paid only a quarter apiece for her drinks and had the consolation of cutting her losses. A band and a dance floor helped the newly matched couples to work off their inhibitions.

Ellen and I took a small table and had not finished our first round before a beefy man approached wearing an executive suit and an expression of friendly stupidity. He asked me to dance. I hadn't expected to hook the first fish, and I feared that Ellen would be put off by my success. Reluctantly, I decided to throw him back.

"I'd like to, but the music is too fast for me," I said in all candor. "Can you come back when they play something slower?"

I felt certain that he would never return, but when the next slow set began, he presented himself again at our table and swept me onto the dance floor. His name was Freddie, and he was one of a party of five General Motors executives in town for a convention. Alfie's always drew a lot of conventioners, and I was content with this one. He was large enough for me to be able to cuddle against him, my cheek on his collarbone, and enjoy the strength and security he afforded. So this was what it was like to feel submissive and female! It was a delicious sensation. I wriggled closer into his arms and began to think about the times I had danced and held girls as he now held me. They had used certain tricks to inflame the male appetite, and I wondered whether I could work the same techniques.

I turned my face up to his and peeked at him shyly from beneath half-lowered lashes. He responded with a superior smile and clutched me more tightly about the waist to convey muscular dominance. Idly I ran a fingertip across the back of his neck. His eyes lit up with animal cunning as he began to convince himself that tonight he would score. As if by accident, I allowed my lips to stray close to his right ear, and I exhaled little puffs of hot air against his earlobe. This appeared to set him afire; he clamped his entire body against mine from clavicles to knee joints, to give me adequate evidence of the height of his arousal. Again I looked up at him, but now my eyes were wide and startled—like a fawn's. He bent and kissed me on the lips, wetly.

It was like operating a machine.

Mercifully, the dance now ended and he led me docilely back to my table, his fingers laced intimately in mine. Ellen had also bagged one of the General Motors quintet, dressed like mine in corporate blue. I had seen them gyrating near us on the dance floor and noticed Ellen observing my conduct incredulously. We exchanged furtive smiles.

"Why don't you girls join us at our table." It wasn't a question but an executive command. Ellen and I uttered ineffectual little protests, gathered our purses, and permitted ourselves to be led off into captivity. In our silly, impractical, feminine way, we forgot all about our tab, knowing that our protectors would take care of everything.

The General Motors executives were all medium-well stewed, but not so stewed as to be incapable of elementary arithmetic, and plainly five of them were too many for two of us. Their leader, a florid, rat-faced little man named Charlie, transmitted a secret message to the two low men in the hierarchy, who wordlessly vanished for the rest of the night. My Freddie having been one of the exiles, Charlie moved in and appropriated me for himself.

After one round of drinks, Charlie proposed that we adjourn for dinner to Chez Paul, one of Chicago's costliest restaurants and a favorite of the expense-account set. Their car, he added grandly, was waiting at the door. And it was—a company-owned Cadillac with a company-paid chauffeur at the wheel. Charlie arranged us all in the car and told the chauffeur where to go and how to get there. At Chez Paul he was just as imperious, addressing captains and waiters with consummate arrogance. The staff repaid him with interest. How they scorned him! And because Ellen and I were in his company, they scorned us too.

But I was determined to wring the last drop of pleasure from this adventure. Worshipfully I looked at Charlie and asked, "Oooh, can we have champagne?" I sounded like an inane featherbrain, and Charlie was taken in by my improvisation.

"A bottle of champagne," he ordered. "And don't give us any of that cheap stuff, either. I want the best—you know, the kind with the red diagonal stripe on the label."

The wine steward presented the bottle for Charlie's approval, his expression at once obsequious and derisive. Charlie tasted it to see if it was corked, making a great show of rolling it on his tongue and lifting his eyes in concentration. He signified his approval with a tiny nod, and the first full glass was poured for me.

"Oooh, it tickles!" I announced gleefully.

Ellen glared at me in outrage.

The menus were dealt around the table, and I studied mine irresolutely. "Charlie, may I order beef Wellington? Please?" I had never dared order it before because as a man I would have had to pay for it, and it is expensive. Now all the cash reserves of General Motors lay ready to gratify my slightest whim. Never had I possessed such power as I wielded that night.

Intoxicated by liquor and admiration, Charlie grew more expansive as dinner wore on. After coffee and liqueurs, he directed us back into the company limousine and returned us to Alfie's for more dancing. I excused myself and went to the ladies' room to repair my face. I had been worrying a good deal that my makeup might wear off or my wig slip out of alignment and reveal the male reality beneath my female façade. That would have made Charlie very angry.

With lipstick and powder refreshed, and confident that everything was in its proper place, I walked out of the ladies' room. Charlie was waiting for me in the shadows. He lunged at me, grappled me ardently, and pressed passionate kisses on me, his tongue probing implacably deeper. He really was a strong little weasel, drunk though he was, and I had a hell of a time fighting for my honor. For his part, Charlie felt cheated. He had spent a considerable amount of General Motors money on me, and he felt entitled. As a man, I could sympathize with him; after all, a deal is a deal. But as a woman, I felt he presumed too much; why couldn't we just be friends?

When Charlie and his colleagues perceived at last that they could not take us by storm, they drove us home, pawing and kissing us like adolescents as we went. Outside our apartment—the marital domicile of an eminent newspaperman and his wife—they kissed us good-night, and Ellen and I went inside, where we compared experiences and laughed until we hurt.

"What did it feel like—you know—to be kissed by a man?" Ellen asked.

"I liked it," I said without hesitation.

And then we fell asleep in each other's arms.

Improbable though it sounds, I still didn't suppose that there was anything seriously askew with my sexual orientation. I had discovered that I liked to dress like a woman, act like a woman, talk like a woman, be admired and danced with and kissed like a woman, but I clung to the belief that these were nothing but manifestations of a far-out transvestism, an exotic flowering of my love for Ellen. With her I was embowered in a private paradise, walled and protected from the world, and my forays into womanhood were merely another bloom of that garden where nothing could hurt us and our happiness would last forever. I did not imagine that I would ever lose Ellen or be forced to leave our Eden.

We continued our expeditions to Alfie's, sometimes picking up men, sometimes not. Usually Ellen made the first catch; she was, after all, twenty years younger than I and far more practiced in feminine wiles. But I won a modest share of conquests. I seemed to exercise a special attraction for fliers: airline pilots, military pilots, retired Air Force pilots. Though none of them wore uniforms, I would discover in the first minutes of conversation that they were aviators. Some sixth sense, I guess. And I had always had a weakness for airplanes and the men who flew them.

One in particular caught my affection. His name was Bob, and he was a first officer on American Airlines—a tall, handsome man who looked like Billy Graham and hummed softly as we danced.

Bob was vulnerable. I had always thought of other men as immune to the weaknesses that lurked inside me, nor had I supposed in my charade as a woman that I had the same strength to offer them as Ellen gave me. But in Bob I glimpsed a loneliness, a need for comfort so desperate that I wanted to hold him and keep him safe. It was a new emotion, something I had never experienced with Charlie or the other self-assured world-beaters who had moved in on me at Alfie's. Bob wanted to take me back to his room in the

Sheraton-Chicago Hotel and go to bed with me. Men invariably wanted to go to bed with the girls they picked up in Alfie's, and I had become accustomed to fending them off with a well-rehearsed story about a messy divorce and fears of upsetting my painfully won emotional tranquillity. But I wanted to go to bed with Bob, not out of any sexual urge but out of a desire to solace him, to cradle his sad and beautiful head in my arms and tell him that everything would be all right.

It was, of course, inconceivable. I could never go to bed with Bob because I lacked the anatomy to gratify him. Merely to reveal the masculinity that lay concealed beneath my skirt would have appalled him and shamed me.

I walked with him hand in hand back to the Sheraton-Chicago. We stood on the sidewalk of Michigan Avenue and kissed while he pleaded and I refused. Presently he put me in a taxi, and as I pulled out into traffic I looked back. He was walking dejectedly into the hotel, head down, hands deep in the pockets of his raincoat, looking lonely and disconsolate. And I was washed by seas of guilt.

Alfie's never seemed the same again. I met Bob there once more, and again he pleaded with me to sleep with him. But this time after I again turned him down, he did not ask me to walk back to his hotel with him.

My luck had run out. I was no longer content to be in a position of defrauding the men who paid for my drinks. If I could not sleep with them, I would not accept their favors. At first, I had taken an exultant satisfaction from claiming the privileges of womanhood. Now I had come to see myself as a deadbeat, running up bills I couldn't pay. It had been fun and it had been easy, but it wasn't honest, and I wasn't going to do it anymore.

EIGHT

Five days a week I continued to play the role of newspaper-man, dressed in Brooks Brothers tweed sport jacket, regimental striped tie, and an Army belt with brass buckle. The snail-paced process of eradicating my beard had begun and I was judiciously plucking my eyebrows, but neither was noticed. In every physical respect I remained a man.

It was decided at the *Tribune* that I should become their man in the Middle East. No one ever made clear to me how this decision was reached; perhaps it stemmed from my experience as a combat correspondent. But it was not a wise decision for several reasons, quite apart from my secret life as a woman. I was a magazine writer by temperament and talent, a type of journalist markedly different from a news reporter. I had no interest in geopolitics or diplomacy, no grasp of international strategy or intrigue, and I hated to travel. Moreover I was far too settled in domestic bliss to exchange it for squalid hotel rooms with inoperative plumbing, frenetic airports, and overbearing customs officials.

But Ellen urged me to accept the assignment. She had

lived in Europe as a student and would happily have abandoned nursing school to return there if I should get a permanent post overseas. And to become a foreign bureau chief would crown my career. In the newspaper business, subordinate editors may rise from rank to rank, becoming eventually managing editor or even, like Kirkpatrick, editor in chief. Writers have no comparable ladder. Their rewards are subtler: a Pulitzer Prize, a citation in *Time* magazine, or a foreign bureau. I was then forty-five. If I was ever going to make my mark as a man, it must be now.

But I was more concerned with making my mark as a woman. Ellen and I were working on a fall suit for me: a rusty-orange plaid skirt with box pleats in front and a matching long-sleeved jacket. It was a difficult project, far beyond my own skills as a seamstress. It lay on top of the dining room sideboard, the pieces cut out but still pinned to the pattern paper. My instinct was to remain in paradise and finish my suit, but sensibly I knew that I must go to the Middle East, and finally I agreed to take the assignment on a five-week trial—three in Egypt and two in Israel. Ellen promised to finish the suit while I was gone.

Cairo is a tough beat to cover at the best of times, and in August it is murder. Moreover the Russians were beginning to pull out of Egypt, and the Egyptians, having suffered a humiliating defeat at the hands of the Israelis, and now smarting from disillusionment with the Russians, treated American journalists with suspicion. No doubt aware, as I was not, that CIA agents were masquerading under the cover of American press credentials, they watched me with simmering hostility.

From the beginning my affairs went badly. The heat was

oppressive, the flies worse, and the food unspeakable. At every turning I confronted sullen Egyptian soldiers, armed with mean-looking submachine guns held ready across their chests. Whenever I passed them, in the street or in the corridors of government buildings, I felt the hair rise on the back of my neck, as if at any moment and for any excuse—if perhaps I failed to heed an order barked at me in Arabic or reached for a cigarette at the wrong moment—they would stitch me across the belly. Or they might simply throw me in jail, hold me incommunicado, forgotten by our own diplomatic staff and eventually by the Egyptian authorities. Anywhere in the United States I knew that the *Tribune* could come to my rescue; in Egypt the *Tribune*'s strength would avail me nothing.

Vietnam had never scared me as Egypt did. I was softer now and less reckless with my own life. While once I had flirted with the release of death, now I passionately wanted to live. Moreover, Vietnam had offered the support of an American environment: The troops I lived with, the food I ate, the officers club where I spent my leisure time, the aircraft that transported me, the Army public relations men who advised me—all were American. Egypt was foreign, ominous.

I registered my routine requests for interviews with the foreign minister and other high officials and settled down to await the government's decision. To occupy the time and maintain communications with my paper, I wrote about anyone I could find who would talk to me—camel drivers, shopkeepers, airline clerks. I thought it an innocuous pastime, but the Egyptians took a different view. I had been advised that my room in the Nile Hilton would be bugged, my telephone tapped. But now I was tailed whenever I went out. A villainous-looking Arab big enough to break me in half would follow me no more than twelve paces behind, and when I entered a bar he would boldly take a seat three stools away. They searched my room and stole my papers—duplicates of stories I had already filed with the censor. They telephoned me at three in the morning and tried to blackmail me into appearing on a propaganda radio program, hinting crudely that I would not get my interview with the foreign minister unless I went along with them.

After a week of this harassment, I complained at the American Embassy, more precisely the American Interests Section of the Spanish Embassy, since the United States did not maintain official diplomatic relations with Egypt at the time. The State Department man who saw me was understanding. Yes, he had heard about me; no, he was not at all surprised by what was happening to me.

But why? I asked. What had I done to annoy them?

As he understood it, I had been talking to camel drivers and shopkeepers, a practice that set me apart from other correspondents. I had made myself conspicuous. I asked what I could do to ingratiate myself with the authorities. There was nothing I could do, he said. If I chose to take his advice, strictly off the record and as one fellow American to another, I would get out of Egypt on the next plane.

I was frightened. But more than that, I was angry. The *Tribune* was spending thousands of dollars to put me on the scene in Egypt, and so far I had scarcely caught a glimpse of a Russian or talked to any government official. If I left now, I would go in failure and disgrace. So I determined to stay.

I was terribly lonely. Although I had established outside communications through the Reuters bureau and was filing copy there daily, I had received no word from Chicago, either from my paper or from Ellen. I did not even know if my copy was getting through. Two and three times a day I stopped at the desk of the Nile Hilton to ask for mail. Nothing. Day after day, nothing. I grew frantic from isolation and a sense of persecution. The sun blazed down relentlessly. Compounding my misery, I became ill with dysentery. At night I would awake, torn with cramps, and find that I had soiled my bed. I would then have to arise and wash my sheets in the bathroom lest the Arab housekeeping staff know that the American correspondent had messed in his bed like a baby.

In the bathroom, too, I studied my face in the mirror. My beard was beginning to grow again. I watched it as a leper might watch encrustations invading his healthy skin. For a year I had been going to an electrologist an hour a week to remove it. That damned beard! No matter how closely I shaved, in six hours time it would show its dark shadow on my face. In Chicago I had had to time my public appearances like Cinderella, always conscious of the clock, knowing that in six hours I would have to scuttle into hiding like a fugitive. Ellen and I had come to refer to this phenomenon as "turning back into a pumpkin." Each whisker burned out at the roots had seemed like a tiny step toward salvation. But the male beard is a resilient foe and for each whisker deleted, another lies in dormancy and will appear weeks later. It takes years to eradicate it all. And there in my Cairo hotel room, I saw the enemy appearing day by day, reasserting my damnable male identity.

I stayed the ordained three weeks in Cairo, out of obstinacy, then retreated to a resort hotel in Famagusta on the island of Cyprus for a few days to try to recover from my dysentery. I did the two weeks in Israel and flew home, missing my connection in Amsterdam and arriving in Chicago ill, exhausted, and shattered.

Ellen met me at the door of our apartment. I clung to her as if I could suck the strength from her body, kissing and kissing that adored face, feeling those beloved shoulders beneath my hands. I wept from relief and joy and love. And then, just before we tumbled into bed to make ardent love, I took one quick look around the apartment, inspecting the walls of my Eden. The pieces of the rusty-orange suit lay just as I had left them atop the dining room sideboard. Ellen had not touched them. I was wildly happy to be home, but I knew the walls of paradise had begun to crack.

"I'm not going to stand for it anymore," Ellen announced the next morning. "I married a man, not a woman. And I don't want to be married to a woman. I'm not a lesbian."

I sympathized with her anguish. "All right, I'll never be Nancy again."

I put away my skirts and dresses and wigs, but significantly I didn't throw them out. During those harrowing weeks in the Middle East when I had received no letters, I had clung to the vision of resuming our sweet, comfortable life together, sometimes as sisters, sometimes as man and wife. I did not think that I could survive without the feminine part of it, but I preferred to try to live on Ellen's terms than to live without her.

Besides, I was too ill to fight her. I hadn't recovered from the dysentery, and day after day I remained in bed, physically debilitated and emotionally tormented by renunciation of life as a woman. Ellen let me stew there until she saw that I lacked the strength and the will to heal myself. Then she got a doctor for me, and in time I returned to work. A few weeks later, tired of my brooding and pouting, she submitted to my resumption of life as Nancy.

Not that she had to tolerate me constantly as a woman.

Five mornings a week I put on my Sears, Roebuck boxer-style underpants, my button-down shirt, my ribbed socks with elasticized tops. Sometimes we went adventuring as man and wife. Once we camped for a week in the Rockies, and once we went cruising with another couple in a twenty-four-foot sailboat.

But increasingly we traveled as sisters. A few weeks after I began to take estrogens, we went to Miami Beach, where I appeared at poolside for the first time in my new persona dressed in a bathing suit. It was a baby-blue print with a small skirt and came equipped with rubber cups to create the impression of a bust, which I lacked at the time. I had to wear a wig, of course, and there was a good deal of apprehension as I crammed my head plus its attendant wig into a bathing cap before entering the pool. There was even more apprehension upon emerging as I peeled off the bathing cap without at the same time peeling down to my crew cut in front of the assembled sunbathers.

There was no such hazard when we took our next trip the following summer to San Francisco, Los Angeles, and Las Vegas. I had been letting my hair grow, bringing it forward in bangs to cover the bald places. Ellen had been setting it on hot rollers and sometimes trimming it. But in Los Angeles she decreed that it had grown beyond her hair dressing ability. It was time for me to learn how to conduct myself in a beauty parlor. She instructed me in the etiquette of tipping—fifty cents to the shampoo girl and two dollars to the hairdresser—and we went to the shop in the Beverly Wilshire Hotel, which struck me as a classy place for my induction into this rite of womanhood.

Ellen was as nervous as a cat for fear that I would commit some breach and disgrace us both, but I was totally self-confident and happy. Whereas as a man I had always felt ill at ease in a barbershop, from the very beginning I was comfortable in beauty shops, confident that this was where I rightly belonged. This curious reaction has carried over to other rituals. I used to sweat with apprehension while trying on a pair of trousers in a men's store, but I have never experienced the slightest unease while trying on skirts and dresses in a women's store. After all the scientific explanations—whether physical or psychological—there remains the inexplicable fact that the male transsexual feels altogether more comfortable as a woman in a woman's world.

The man at the Beverly Wilshire gave me a darling set with lots of teasing in the crown, and I walked out jubilantly. Ellen said I had talked too much and was greatly relieved to get me away from there. She tended to worry more than I did about my ladylike deportment and laid down a hundred strictures on my behavior. (Don't look at the displays in the windows of men's clothing stores, don't tell a taxi driver what route to take.)

When we got to Las Vegas, I displayed an unwonted independence by going alone to the beauty shop across the street from the Stardust Hotel. This time the hairdresser built in an enormous amount of teasing, glued into place with lots of hair spray. I emerged looking like a whore—an expensive whore, I hoped. That night I put on a long skirt and long-sleeved Qiana blouse and walked slinkily through the gambling casinos, feeling like a femme fatale. For the first time, I caught an inkling of what it might be like to be mistress of my own fate.

That was important. From the beginning, my life as a woman had been largely the product of Ellen's hands and instruction. She had made my clothes or helped me to buy them, had done my hair, chaperoned me in bars, taught me to dance, tutored me in proper conduct. My gratitude was beginning to yield to impatience at my dependence on her. I was, after all, well past forty years old, and I wanted to succeed or fail as a woman in my own right, on my own responsibility.

I had proved during our evenings at Alfie's that I could be accepted as a woman by men, but what did they know? Few men are perceptive judges of women, although all like to think they are. The true test of my femininity, I knew, lay in the eyes of other women. So I enrolled that summer in a shorthand class that met every Saturday afternoon at the Central YMCA Community College. Ellen couldn't help me there. For the first and, as it has turned out, only time, I was frightened about passing as a woman. Surely in that classroom of twenty women, someone would detect a flaw in my clothes, my makeup, my physique. I could imagine the shriek of horrified discovery, the accusing finger pointed, the steely grip of the security guard as I was flung out of the building. I could never bring this off. Men might accept me, but women never.

I could have spared myself the anxiety. The only aspect of the class that held any concern for me, and that soon passed, was the recitation. No matter how much the transsexual may indulge in surgery and hormones—and I had had neither yet—the voice does not change except to the extent that it can be altered by simulation and practice. In its natural state, my voice was distressingly male; I had sung bass in the choir for years. But the difference in vocal range between men and women is generally not as great as one might suppose. Equally important differences lie in musicality, intonation, and what might be called didacticism. Men hand down pronouncements when they speak; women suggest and question. Men are forthright and sensible; women are just silly little things. (This is not my own wisdom but was imparted to me by a woman speech therapist whose own voice happened to be pitched rather low. She said that if she telephoned to make an airline reservation and knew exactly what she wanted, she was addressed as "sir," but if she was vague and woolly-headed, she was addressed as "ma'am." I profited by her counsel and have hardly ever been called "sir" on the telephone.)

My classmates in shorthand class accepted me as just one of the girls. They welcomed me during coffee breaks and invited me to practice dictation with them at home. But the decisive test came in the ladies' room.

Male transsexuals typically worry a good deal about venturing into the ladies' room, wanting to go there more than anyplace in the world and yet terrified of being discovered. I confess I never had much of a problem. Ellen introduced me to this mystery, as she did so many others. She took me into the ladies' room at Marshall Field's, and it was no big deal, really. Women cherish a far greater sense of privacy than men. Women retire into booths and bolt the door. Men belly up to a row of urinals in virile companionship, then turn while stuffing themselves back into their pants and zipping up their flies without a shred of modesty. As a man I had died a thousand deaths when I tried to perform in this environment; as a woman I found it the easiest thing in the world.

My confidence was clinched one Saturday when my shorthand instructor confronted me in the ladies' room and borrowed a dime for the Kotex machine, then poured out her heart in the most intimate revelations about her menstrual difficulties and the problems of her sex life. I was sympathetic, and I like to think she felt better for having had a shoulder to cry on.

The truth was that the world was accepting me far more readily as a woman than it ever had as a man, and this despite four decades and more of the most arduous exertion to establish my male self. As a woman I was freely granted everything that I had sought vainly as a man: friendship, approval, laughter, sympathy. I was delighted to have these things now, though slightly put out that they had been withheld from me before.

Best of all, I was beginning to approve of myself. I looked at my face in the mirror, the face of a man who dressed up in drag, who danced with other men and kissed them in a way that anyone aware of my anatomic sex would unhesitatingly label homosexual, a man who was taking the most frightful risks with an ideal marriage, who almost daily stood in danger of arrest for violating the city's cross-dressing ordinance—I looked at this face and smiled and said, "I like you." It was a novel experience.

If I liked my new self better, Ellen liked it considerably less. The stresses imposed by my mutation were eroding the metal of our marriage, and sometimes it would crack, especially under external pressure. In the middle of my secretarial education, we took a three-week trip to Europe, and it went badly from the start. Ellen bought the airplane tickets and had them made out in the names of "Mr. and Mrs. Hunt." At first she said she had done it absentmindedly, then she explained she had been unable to admit to the travel agent that she was not going with her husband. Months later, she confessed she had done it on purpose to force me to go as a man. I had no intention of traveling through Europe disguised as a man, and for days we fought bitterly about the matter.

London had never looked so lovely as it did that June. We explored it endlessly by tube and on foot with Ellen as always managing the map and plotting our itinerary. We took the train to Kew and wandered all day among those immacuately groomed gardens, half narcotized by the sweet smells and gentle sun. We went by boat down the Thames to the maritime museum at Greenwich and attended Covent Garden to see a glittering performance of *Cosi fan Tutte*. We strolled among the ancient colleges of Oxford, dined on roast beef and Yorkshire pudding at the Gilbert and Sullivan Pub, and explored a small Christopher Wren church not far from Fortnum & Mason. We joined the tourists at Westminster Abbey and walked from there to the changing of the guard, where we had a bruising argument.

We cruised for a week down the Avon from Stratford in a narrow boat, a kind of floating hotel. We crossed in a channel steamer to the Hook of Holland, sharing a stateroom with two pretty Belgian girls, and proceeded by train to Amsterdam, where we had a dreadful row in a restaurant.

"You're ruining this trip for both of us," I stormed when we got outside, "and I'm damned well not going to put up with it."

We were sitting on a bench beside a canal, and my feet hurt from walking the cobbled streets in heels.

Ellen nodded miserably. "I know," she conceded. "What do you want to do about it?"

"If you don't cut it out, I'm going to go back to Chicago and I don't care what you do so long as you stay the hell out of my sight."

I was being harsh less from conviction than from a sense of duty. Ellen had occasionally instigated quarrels to provoke me into asserting my male dominance, at no real risk to herself since she could easily win a fight with me if she chose to. It was a kind of injection she sometimes required. But now the medication did not relieve her. She needed to be mastered by a man, not by this epicene person in ruffled blouse and cornflower skirt who sat with her beside the canal in Amsterdam. The old talismans were failing.

We took a train to Bonn, where we saw the house in which Beethoven was born and had a quarrel that lasted the better part of two days. We rode a cog railway to the ruined castle of Drachenfels near Königswinter, high above the Rhine. A ski lift carried us to Schloss Rheineck, downstream from Remagen, where we could see the piers of the old Remagen Bridge, whose capture marked a turning point in World War II. We went to Cologne and saw the cathedral and argued fiercely.

By the time we reached Paris, we had both perceived that we couldn't continue at each other's throat. By enormous effort, we established a truce based partly on the memory of our love and partly on the knowledge that a few more days would see us home and release us from the bondage of each other's company. We had been the best of companions on a hundred journeys: on skiing weekends and camping trips, on sailing cruises and motor tours, in the Las Vegas casinos and the Everglades swamps. Now all those journeys lay behind us, and there would never be another.

NINE

I can remember only once when my life has been altered by the printed word. That was upon reading an article in the *New York Times Magazine* on March 17, 1974, by David Holden, a correspondent for the London *Sunday Times*. It described the transition from man into woman of an English journalist now known as Jan Morris.

Several aspects of that article struck me. In the first place, it was written with a sensitivity and understanding uncommon in the field of transsexual literature. Miss Morris did not do better in her own book. Secondly, I was astonished by the similarities between Morris's life and my own: We were almost the same age, both educated in Anglican choir schools, both Army veterans of the last few months of World War II, both graduates of first-rate universities (she went to Oxford and I went to Yale), both journalists, and both known for physical courage (she for covering the first ascent of Mt. Everest, I for combat correspondence). She was a far more eminent writer than I, but our main difference lay in the fact that she had taken female hormones and eventually had undergone sex-reassignment surgery, two irrevocable steps I had scarcely considered. And yet, if Morris could do it, why not I?

The *Tribune* had sent me back to the *Sunday Magazine,* no longer as a writer but as an editor. I had by now refused further overseas assignment, failed as a city reporter, failed again as a writer for the women's feature sections. I despised the ritual method of reporting the news, which typically requires attendance at a morning press conference through which the newspaper people suffer while the television people illuminate the occasion with quartz lamps and inane questions, and I abominated the standard form of the newspaper story.

At first I was glad to be back on the *Sunday Magazine,* where for a dozen years I had enjoyed professional success. I even took a sour satisfaction from being made an editor instead of a writer. I had exhausted the emotional resources necessary to the kind of magazine writing on which I had built my reputation. In those articles I had wept for young widows, bereaved mothers, leukemic children, disillusioned cops, frightened soldiers. I had no more tears left. The raw places from which I had wrung so much anguish for the involvement of my readers had crusted over and formed calluses.

But equally, I discovered, I lacked the knack to become an executive editor. Doggedly I toiled with galley proofs, production schedules, and page layouts, doing an adequate job only by great exertion. I had no calling for it, no flair. Furthermore, a disease had sickened the morale of the entire staff since I had last worked with them, and I was soon infected.

The cause lay mostly in the magazine's editor, a man whose talents I did not come to appreciate fully until long after we had parted in animosity. He had been a good friend to me for many years, had created the environment in which I could flourish as a writer, and had even stood as godfather for my youngest daughter. His marriage was now coming unglued, and he had become brooding and sullen—almost menacing. He had turned over the management of the magazine to a young protégée whom we all disliked, a woman incompetent to take over the magazine's flight controls. I had always had a horror of office politics and had invariably handled them badly when foolish enough to try. Still, as a sort of executive editor I was obligated to my associates, so when I had run out of all other remedies, I became an informer. I later learned I was not the first. Two others on the magazine staff had also reported to the editor's superior. Nevertheless, he allowed his protégée to continue in the pilot's seat, yanking manically at the controls. It was a nightmare flight.

But outside Tribune Tower, living almost entirely as a woman, I was in a state of perfect joy. I had come to recognize that manhood with all its trappings and duties was intolerable. I loathed my crew-cut hair, my tweeds and flannels, my clumsy rubber-soled Oxfords. I hated the harsh, unyielding cadences of masculine speech I was forced to utter. I had to remember to walk heavily, to drape myself awkwardly in my chair, to prop my feet on my desk. The feminine graces I had merely practiced before had now become habits, and the hearty male deportment, once ingrained, now felt artificial, a laborious bit of playacting.

Morris had faced this dilemma and solved it, and given the courage and resolution, so could I. Morris had taken hormones, and so could I. (I knew the very doctor who would prescribe them for me, just down the corridor from my electrologist.) Morris had gone to Dr. Harry Benjamin in New York, starting down the road that would end on the operating table, and I could do that too.

But to pursue such a course I would have to risk my life with Ellen, which I valued as highly as my sense of feminine gender. The hormones in time would make me impotent. The surgery would require breaking the legal tie of marriage. I did not think that I could face life without Ellen, and so I did not think about it at all. I assumed it would work out satisfactorily one way or another because the alternative was inconceivable. Without Ellen there could be no happiness.

But equally, there could be neither happiness nor life itself without my own existence as a woman. Two days after I had read the article about Jan Morris, I wrote to Harry Benjamin and asked for help. Then I went to get hormone shots.

The doctor was a harassed man in a cluttered office that stank of urine. He treated a great many transsexuals.

"Why do you want these shots?" he asked me dubiously.

I didn't know how to answer him. Because I wanted to feel more like a woman? Because I wanted to grow breasts? Because the shots symbolized a turning point, the renunciation of one gender and adoption of the other? Because I wanted to discover what estrogens would feel like and do to me? Because a lonely American Airlines pilot had asked me to go to bed with him? How could I tell any of these things to this preoccupied old man?

"I believe I'm a transsexual," I said, "and I think these hormone shots will help me to know for sure."

"You're aware that they'll make you impotent?"

"How long before that happens?"

"Six months, a year at most."

"That's all right, then. I'll know before six months."

"I won't let you have them until I've given you a complete physical examination."

"Good, I ought to have a physical anyway."

And so it was settled. He gave me a physical and followed with an injection of estrogens in the buttocks. I knew that I had crossed a river and would never go back. I left his office afloat on a cloud of elation.

"You look like the cat that swallowed the canary," Ellen observed later over cocktails at home.

I knew I was smiling irrepressibly. I felt suffused with a contentment that originated only partly in the mind. Already the estrogens were affecting me physically. I could feel my genitalia shrinking in a way men commonly experience when they swim in cold water. The hated mark that the gods had put upon me was receding. I felt absolutely marvelous.

So immediate was the impact of that first injection that I almost expected to undergo an overnight metamorphosis, like a grub turning into a butterfly. Optimistically, I began to measure my body once a week, entering my findings in a shorthand notebook under the headings of "Date," "Bust," "Waist," and "Hips." I still have that record. The first date, March 22, 1974, notes a bust of 33½ inches, a waist of 29¼, and hips of 34¼—hardly an hourglass figure. My height was a shade under 5' 11", and my weight hovered around 133. Within a week, my bust had grown a quarter of an inch; in two weeks it had increased slightly more than half an inch. At the end of five weeks, I had gained an inch and a quarter in the bust and half an inch around the hips. I was enchanted with this marvel wrought by the American pharmaceutical industry.

After that, however, my progress slowed to a more sedate

pace. At the end of a year, I had achieved a thirty-six-inch circumference in both bust and butt, and there I leveled off. Surgeons still inquire solicitously if I wouldn't like to have some nice breast implants, and while I admit I have given the matter some thought, I always reply that I am resigned to being a skinny, flat-chested broad. Most transsexuals, including my friend Miss Johnson in the University of Virginia hospital, elect to have implants.

The physical effects of estrogen ingestion do not stop with breasts and buttocks. In the course of two years, my entire musculature has been affected. My wrists have grown so slender that watchbands which once fit snugly now flop about. My shoulders, which once sloped steeply down from the neck, have assumed a feminine squareness; bra and shoulder-bag straps no longer slide off. My neck and arms have grown thinner as the underlying muscles have diminished. As one would expect, this loss of muscle tissue has meant a comparable loss of brute strength. I can no longer haul my window air conditioner or lift an upholstered chair. Women *are* weaker than men, and I have had to accustom myself to the difference.

As I lost muscle, I gained fat. The breasts, of course, are mostly fatty tissue and mine are now as subject to cancer as any other woman's; when I go to the doctor, I am routinely subjected to a breast examination. The facial fat has migrated, leaving the lower cheeks a flatter plane and building up over the cheekbones. The sinews of the legs, which once stood out like cords, are now clad in subcutaneous fat. Even the armpits, once so deep that they were difficult to shave, have shoaled with fat.

The very smell of one's body alters under the influence of estrogens. "You used to have such a nice, manly smell,"

Ellen often lamented toward the end of our life together. "I miss it."

But I didn't miss it. I exulted in my changes. Smiling constantly, I gloried in the secret, subtle transformation from hard, angular man into soft, molded woman. My burden of self-loathing lightened day by day.

No one inside Tribune Tower suspected how I was changing. To them I remained the same remote, prickly man clad in the same white button-down shirt and gray flannels, staring coldly through the same heavy-rimmed eyeglasses. I would no more have revealed my joy to them than I would have bared my newly pink and everted nipples. My change remained my secret.

Estrogens could not rid me of every vestige of my male inheritance. Some of them—my height, my heavy jaw—I would have to accept with as much grace as I could muster. My beard I could eradicate through electrolysis, and indeed I almost had. I could not cure my nearsightedness, but I could replace my eyeglasses with contact lenses, a noticeable improvement. (Vainly, I like to think that my eyes are one of my better features.)

The hair remained a problem. I had been letting my crew cut grow out, and with the hormone shots its texture had become finer and less wiry. But no injectable substance known to me could reseed those bald patches on either side of my widow's peak. For that I would need hair transplants, a step I was inexplicably reluctant to take. After six months, my hair was long enough so that I could comb it into bangs and so discard the wigs I wore as a woman. But I dreaded walking in the street lest a wind lift my concealing bangs and reveal my baldness to passersby.

In time I bowed my head to the demands of beauty and

went to a doctor for hair transplants. It's a relatively simple in-office procedure; many doctors have their assistants do the actual work. They dig little plugs of hair out of the back of the head, where there is plenty to spare, and stick them into holes that they have dug in the bald places. Each plug cost me $12, and I got ninety-five of them in the course of two visits for a total of $1,140. Best money I ever spent. Within six months they were flourishing like weeds, and at the end of a year I feared no wind that blew.

But I could not reconcile myself to sex-reassignment surgery. My health was blooming under the estrogens, my mood was euphoric. Why let some hack surgeon have at me with a knife and ruin everything? Moreover, I couldn't see that I had any practical need for a vagina. Though I had been elated to discover that I could arouse a man, had even felt some physical response in myself, my abhorrence of homosexuality curtailed any wish to be able to perform as a woman.

So a vagina seemed somehow superfluous. I had no dread of the operation; neither did I have any late compunction about shedding my male genitalia. But I did feel that I should have a compelling and rational argument for stretching myself supine on the operating table.

Society provided enough such reasons, heaven knows. If I continued to dress as a woman while retaining my male anatomy, I would be living outside the law, subject to arrest and disgrace on half a dozen counts. But if I joined the select company of "postsurgical transsexuals," I could change my birth certificate and my driver's license and live free of any legal sanctions. The operation might wreck me physically and emotionally, but for society's purposes I would be saved. Somehow this prospect lacked the power to move me toward the table.

Still, even as I pondered and agonized, I expected that I would undergo surgery later if not sooner. I could plot the events of my transition on a graph and establish a line of progress like the parabolic curve in a calculus problem. By a combination of metaphysical computations and guesswork, I could project that curve until it crossed the anatomical x axis. If the solution to this equation failed to reach me in the marrow of my bones, my mind's eye could still see that graph. I had not progressed far enough to cross the axis, but I knew I would.

I had been taking estrogens for about a month when my newspaper career nearly toppled about me. I had been squabbling with the magazine editor intermittently for several months. We had it out one evening that spring—he and I in his corner office with the fine view up Michigan Avenue—and ended the feud like gentlemen, with assurances of mutual regard and promises to work for the restoration of friendship. His next move was a classic of speed, surprise, and duplicity. He arrived at Tribune Tower the following morning unusually early for him, went directly to Kirkpatrick, and asked to have me removed from the magazine. Kirkpatrick obliged him at once, and I was informed that my future on the paper, if indeed I had any, would be in another department.

I don't know what I would have done if I hadn't been turning into a woman at the time; I suspect something manly and stupid. Instead, I put on my best skirt and blouse and went downtown to answer a classified ad for a secretarial position at the McGraw-Hill publishing company. No résumé was required, and the application blank obliged me to tell almost no lies apart from omitting my college education—a woman, after all, could not have gone to Yale in my day, except in graduate school. But the blank did stipulate in bold type that a physical examination would be required as a condition of employment, and I was scarcely in a position to undergo that. So I knew I was beaten before I started.

That was a pity, too, because they loved me there, and for good reason: In the typing test, on an unfamiliar machine, I scored seventy-five words a minute. I couldn't believe it—line after line of perfect typing flowing from my fingers at lightning speed. I had never typed so well before.

They offered me my choice of two secretarial positions and telephoned me at home for months afterward to tempt me with others, but the pay was terrible—just enough to cover my alimony with nothing left over for me. Furthermore, as they outlined my proposed duties—letters to type, ledgers to post, switchboards to run—it sounded unspeakably dreary. After all my training in shorthand class to join the secretarial ranks of womanhood, I found there was a limit to what I would endure for my adopted sex. But with no admissible college record, employment history, or references, I could ask for nothing better. The most probable story I could invent had me as a divorced housewife newly returning to the labor market. I would have to start at the bottom of the ladder, and at the age of forty-six, I would never get far above the first rung.

Transsexuals routinely face this dilemma. With their surgery completed, just as they are adjusting to their new gender, they move to new towns, adopt new names, make new friends, start new careers. I supposed that someday I would have to do the same, to make out as best I could as, say, a clerk-typist for a hardware company in Youngstown, Ohio. I knew I would be willing to pay that additional price for womanhood, whenever the grim day came, but it wasn't something I could contemplate at the time. The prospect of life apart from the newspaper business—like life without Ellen—paralyzed my reason. I knew I could survive; I just couldn't think how.

But at least I had been offered work as a secretary, and I rejoiced in my acceptance as a woman at the moment the *Tribune* was condemning me as a man. My situation in Tribune Tower was still unclear the day after I'd been pulled off the magazine. The Sunday editor, having received a succession of unfavorable reports from the magazine editor, declared that he had no other job for me anywhere in his department. Next I was summoned before a high-ranking executive known as a hatchet man. He was very severe, and though he did not fire me, he hinted broadly that he was thinking about it.

Finally I came before the managing editor, an Australian of immense charm and wit whom I had always adored.

"I am a patient man," he told me wearily, employing his Oxonian accent to great effect, "but I can be absolutely ruthless." He paused to stab out his cigarette in a manner suggesting the execution of an intractable subordinate.

"Oh Max, please don't talk like that," I pleaded. "You scare me to death." I was looking on him as one of the most attractive men I knew, and I was smiling imbecilely. Poor Max! He would have been horrified had he known the viewpoint from which I now saw him. As it was, he seemed baffled by this odd response from his hard-bitten foreign correspondent. He had expected a dangerous cur to be subdued but instead found himself closeted with an affectionate lapdog. He didn't let it upset him, however, but plunged on gamely.

"You know, you are in very serious trouble," he said, not threatening me now, but plainly concerned.

"That's all right," I told him happily. "I went out job-interviewing yesterday and got two offers."

"From newspapers?" he asked quickly. I still retained something of the reputation of a star, and he would not have wanted the competing *Sun-Times* to get me.

"In publishing," I answered vaguely.

"Well, the question remains, what am I going to do with you?"

It was a serious question, I knew. Bad news travels fast in a place like Tribune Tower, and I had about me the smell of a loser. Suddenly no one remembered my golden decade as a magazine writer, nor the fact that I had won the *Tribune*'s highest editorial prize (good for $850 that year, as I recall) for combat correspondence. They knew only that I had failed in my recent assignments and that now even my own *Sunday Magazine* didn't want me. Both the magazine editor and Kirkpatrick himself—the two men on the paper I had respected most and served best—had repudiated me. Any supervisor would have had to be crazy to take me into his department.

Fortunately, the financial editor was crazy. A warm-hearted and totally fearless Greek who had applauded every word I ever wrote, he had been urging me for years to come to work for him. In fact, he had repeated his offer only two weeks before, when I chanced to meet him in the bank. Now in my extremity, I recalled his invitation. I knew almost nothing about finance and business and cared less, but I needed a sanctuary until the storm blew over, and so I proposed to Max that he make me a financial writer. He looked at me with mild surprise, undoubtedly aware of how unqualified I was for this specialty, but within a week I was covering stockholders' meetings and interviewing bank presidents. I had found my temporary niche among the gargoyles of Tribune Tower.

Safely tucked away with the Dow-Jones ticker and the bound volumes of Standard & Poor's, I embarked upon the final stage of my transition from man to woman, not as an attack upon obstacles, but rather a surrender, a yielding to forces that had wearied me and broken my resistance. I assumed that it would eventually cost me both my job and my marriage, but similarly I assumed that one day I would die. I couldn't help one any more than the other. My fall from corporate grace had taught me how quickly and capriciously my *Tribune* career could be demolished. It made no sense, then, to deny myself a comparatively permanent identity, at least not for the sake of a job that could be snatched away in a minute.

And so I put my job at risk along with my home, my family, my professional reputation, and my friends. I began to wear women's clothes to the office. At first no one knew they were women's clothes. I started with man-tailored blouses by Judy Bond or Ship 'n Shore. They contrasted sharply with the white Oxford button-downs and regimental-striped ties I had worn since the age of twelve, but they didn't differ much from the floral shirts that many younger men were wearing now, aside from the fact that mine buttoned on the left instead of the right. To my wardrobe of blouses I added women's slacks, most of them made at home with Ellen's help and cunningly styled to stay just inside the bounds of what might be considered acceptable for a man. Again, they contrasted wildly with my previous gray flannels, but they were excused on the grounds of fashion. After all, many middle-aged men go off the deep end with youthful colors and patterns. To wear with the slacks I bought a pair of penny loafers, quite indistinguishable from those that any man might wear, except that mine were manufactured by American Girl. When I later reviewed these shifts with friends who had witnessed them, I learned that while they noticed my suddenly bright plumage, they never guessed the cause.

I thought I looked rather attractive in my office blouses and slacks, but as I inspected myself in the mirror, I had to admit to a pallid blandness of the face, especially about the eyes. A bit of makeup would help a lot, I decided. Nothing obvious, of course; nothing that anyone would notice. Just a subtle dab to heighten the color and accent the contours. And so I began to arrive in the office wearing powder, blusher, and eventually mascara.

Now the whispers began, though I did not hear them then nor learn about them for several months. The women were the first to catch on. The men simply could not believe the evidence of their eyes. I was the combat correspondent, the old hand in the Middle East, the police reporter. I had made a fetish and a profession of manhood. (Indeed I had once written an article on what it means to be a man, and the United States Marine Corps, as a token of respect and appreciation, had given me a bronze paperweight cast in the form of the Marine Corps emblem—the anchor and globe surmounted by an eagle; I have it still on my desk.) The things that were happening to me could not conceivably happen, and so the men discounted them.

Strangers could see perfectly well, of course. At a press conference held by Universal Oil Products, I raised my hand to ask a question and the president of the company said, "Yes, Miss?" Bus drivers and salesclerks were also calling me "Miss." A copy girl mistook me for the financial department secretary. Others had the misdirected kindness to be embarrassed on my behalf when these things happened, but I was inordinately pleased.

I began to wear sweaters to reveal the slightest shadow of my emerging breasts. The effect was a good deal more satisfactory if I wore a bra under the sweater, but I wasn't quite ready to create a scandal. As it was, people were beginning to respond to me subconsciously as a woman, even while still consciously oblivious of my transformation. The secretaries and I chatted frequently about cooking and crocheting, and when we baked cakes or pastries for the office, we traded recipes. Whether they guessed my secret or not, most of these women accepted me uncritically. So I happened to know a lot about dressmaking; they would ask my advice about a tricky placket or show me the fabric they had bought during lunch hour. And if they thought there was anything bizarre in my questions about shampoos and hair conditioners, they kept their opinions to themselves.

Men, when they began to notice, reacted in a variety of ways, depending on how well they knew me and how secure they were in their own virility. Most of my male friends became kinder and more protective, but subtly more distant. I was now less likely than ever to be included in their invitations to lunch or as audience for their dirty jokes. My boss in the financial department, an exceedingly tough cookie who had fought his way up from the bottom in South Chicago, glanced at me distractedly one night as I left for home and said, "Night-night." I could have kissed him. The office manager, a retired Army sergeant major, eyed me with hostility. We had been friends once and used to swap stories about our days as Army noncoms. One of the first men to see what was happening to me, he felt I was selling out the side.

It was he who caused me to retire at last from the men's

room, and I was happy to go. Even locked inside a booth, I felt embarrassed in the men's lavatory, and began to suspect that the men were embarrassed to have me there. One afternoon as I was washing my hands I saw in the mirror the reflection of the office manager behind me. He was staring at me with something more than dislike—he was shocked and outraged by my presence. I retreated hastily from that male bastion and never went back. It took the office manager a full year to swallow his antipathy; now he smiles and forces himself to make small talk with me, a courtesy I value, knowing the effort it has cost him.

Those were delicious days, as poignant as an autumn afternoon that spells the death of summer. I shook with inner laughter at the paradox of my transition, at once so blatant and so unsuspected. I would tiptoe to the edge of open declaration, announcing myself with eyeliner or a bra worn to the office, then skitter away the next day with a necktie and an enormous pair of thick-soled white bucks. I set my hair in rollers, then told profane police-beat stories, snarled from the corner of my mouth. I was playing tag and waiting to be caught.

And of course, they caught me at last. To this day, I don't know which *Tribune* executive first took notice of my odd conduct. No one has ever discussed it with me, though I'm sure they considered me a most distasteful problem. I had assumed from the beginning that they would fire me when they found me out, but I was mistaken.

"I want to put you on the copy desk," the assistant managing editor told me. He had the square, chiseled good looks of an actor. He also had a Pulitzer prize, won for daring and enterprise as a reporter. He was the embodiment of manliness, and I could think of no one in the newsroom less likely to understand the passage on which I was embarked or to sympathize with the winds that drove me. But perhaps he didn't know. He had said nothing about my appearance, after all, and I rejoiced that by chance that day I was wearing gray flannels and an old sweater baggy enough to hide my breasts.

"I don't want to go on the copy desk," I protested. "I'm a writer, not a copy editor." This must be another one of those idiot personnel experiments, I decided, totally unrelated to my womanliness. I could talk my way out of it.

But the man persisted. "We want you on the copy desk."

"Why don't you fire me?" I suggested. If I could persuade him to tie the can to me, the *Tribune* would give me severance pay, which in my case would amount to almost a year's salary.

He shook his head sadly. "I don't want to fire you." He said the words with infinite gentleness. So he knew—he knew after all.

"Let me have the rest of the day to think it over."

"Sure, take off and go think it over."

But there was nothing to think over. I hadn't walked two blocks up Michigan Avenue before I realized that the *Tribune* had decided not to extinguish me like a bug. I would not have to slink off to a strange city, invent a new identity, go to work as a secretary in an unaccustomed business at one-third of my present salary. Whether as man or woman, I could continue to be myself, surrounded by the people I had known for a dozen years, working at the only trade I knew. To sit at the copy desk seemed a small price to pay for this.

Anyway, I was tired of being a writer. I had found the financial beat even more tedious than I had expected, and worse than that, the ambiguity of my gender was complicating my work. To confront a captain of industry—he in businessman blue and I in feminine floral—to conduct an interview while undergoing his amused or speculative scrutiny was becoming increasingly difficult. I could handle an interview as a man, I could probably do it even better as a woman, but I faltered when I was neither one nor the other. The copy desk would remove me from this quandary.

I have never discovered why the *Tribune* didn't fire me, though I've heard a dozen explanations. The most popular holds that, in the prevailing climate of militant feminism, the paper feared that I would bring suit on a charge of sex discrimination. (A transsexual school teacher subsequently fought such a case all the way up to the United States Supreme Court and lost.) Another theory holds that the editors feared a staff rebellion, particularly on the part of the younger women. It is true that some of them became good friends of mine, and a few went so far as to tell me that they admired and respected what I was doing, but I doubt that at the time of my emergence the women of the newsroom would have felt such fierce loyalty to me as to take up arms on my behalf.

I would like to believe that the *Tribune* spared me out of consideration for my skills and past accomplishments, but I have never heard this theory seriously advanced, and I have been forced to discard it as improbable.

My own hunch is that they kept me as a token and an insurance policy. Corporations were being harassed with lawsuits charging employment discrimination, the loss of which was costing them millions. Women, blacks, gays, Latinos—all were dragging businesses into court and suing them down to their socks. Now the *Tribune,* like all progressive companies, was hastening to remedy any past defects by hiring as many qualified women and blacks as it could recruit, and it had made remarkable progress. Already the copy desk was beginning to look like a study hall at Vassar. But to retain a full-blooded transsexual on the staff was to offer the ultimate proof of corporate liberality, a sure defense against any conceivable accusations of prejudice.

And in fact the *Tribune* was committing an act of true liberality. I daily give thanks to a merciful Providence that I wasn't employed by a bank or an insurance company or even some other newspaper, any and all of which, at the first tinge of eye makeup, would have heaved me out into the street.

Yet the Tribune could not make a social success of me in the newsroom. For that I would have to rely on my own resources, and the outcome hung in doubt for some time. A newspaper newsroom operates on a delicately balanced system of intimacies and animosities. Newspaper people devote their professional lives to conveying information, not least among themselves. To speed this exchange, they work close together. The copy desk, for example, is a single piece of furniture—battered with age and prickly with splinters that snag stockings at an awesome rate—at which seven or eight editors may be working shoulder to shoulder. To be separated by half the width of the newsroom constitutes an intolerable gulf for some newspeople, who will then pick up the phone to maintain communication with someone in plain view fifteen feet away. Because their outlook is specialized and their working hours often aberrant, they tend to congregate outside the newsroom as well as inside, particularly at bars. Introducing a sexual anomaly into this finely tuned machine required some daring on the part of management.

I think we were all apprehensive that first afternoon when

I took my seat on the copy-desk rim. I did not know how much they understood about what was happening to me, and I suppose they wondered whether I would go limp-wristed on them and start to chatter in falsetto. Copy desks usually have a great deal of work that must be performed with great accuracy and at high speed. A copy chief controls this flow of work, presiding from the center of the horse-shoe-shaped desk with his subordinate copy editors arrayed around him. (For this reason, the copy chief is called a "slot man"—or, since women now often hold the job, a "slot person"—while the subordinate copy editors are said to be "on the rim.") The slot person deals out news stories to the rim people, who edit and write headlines for them before throwing them back to the slot for approval. As the edition dead-line approaches, the pace becomes frantic. A disruptive personality can wreak havoc on a copy desk. I have seen otherwise adequately qualified copy editors refused further employment after a two-week trial because they created friction.

The copy desk and I soon struck a balance of toleration, thanks in part to my oldest and best male friend, Clarence Petersen. We had met on the *Sunday Magazine* more than a dozen years before, both of us young and each mortally certain of his own wit. We had both become stars, he as the *Tribune*'s television columnist, and both of us had tasted the glory of appearing on TV talk shows and seeing our photographs on the sides of the *Tribune* circulation trucks. We had written a book together once, to our mutual profit and enjoyment. Each of us stood in awe of the other's writing, convinced of the impossibility of attaining the other's felicitous style. Now both of us, through weariness and misfortune, had been brought low to the ignominy of the copy desk, where we figuratively embraced like two exiles in a foreign land.

"What the hell is happening to you?" Pete asked me one day shortly after I had arrived on the desk.

"How do you mean?" I asked innocently.

"Well, you come in here with long hair and those flowery shirts—people are beginning to talk about it."

"I'm turning into a woman," I said.

"Oh—well, okay, I'm glad you told me. Everybody's been asking *me* about it, for Christ's sake!"

Because we were known to be old friends, Pete became my advocate and interpreter. The questions that people dared not ask me, out of misplaced delicacy, they put to Pete, who struggled with them as best he could. Slowly and with Pete's help, I began to win a measure of acceptance.

The process was greatly accelerated, however, by the intervention of the gossip columnist for the competing Chicago *Sun-Times.*

"This is Irv Kupcinet," said the voice on the telephone, awakening me from a nap. In the background I could hear the clatter of dishes and cutlery, and I pictured him calling from his table at the Pump Room.

"Hi, Irv," I said, as if I had known him for years. Had I really known him, I would have remembered that he is called "Kup," not "Irv."

"There's a story going around that you're turning into a woman," he said. "Would you care to comment on that?"

I knew that every newspaper bar in the city of Chicago had been talking about little else for the last month, so I wasn't surprised that Kupcinet had finally stumbled onto it. "I don't think I want to comment on it," I said, "though it's true enough."

"You admit it?" he asked.

"I don't admit it—I state it as a fact. But I'm afraid it won't make much of a story for you because I have to ask you not to use my name."

"Why shouldn't I use your name?" he asked aggressively. Names, after all, are the lifeblood of the gossip columnist.

"Out of professional courtesy, for one thing," I replied, "and because I haven't told my kids yet for another."

Kupcinet disliked this inhibition, and I didn't blame him, but he grudgingly accepted it. On August 1, 1975, he began the second paragraph of his column: "One of Chicago's top newspapermen soon will become a newspaperwoman. He is undergoing a sex change. We trust his friends and co-workers at the *Chicago Tribune* will help him through his ordeal. (We agreed not to reveal his name because members of his family still are not aware of the change.) . . ."

The *Tribune* news staff was outraged. Not only had Kupcinet broken a tacit agreement among all Chicago journalists to maintain silence about me, but he had presumed to tell *Tribune* people how to treat me when they had already been treating me very well indeed. At this effrontery from an outsider, my colleagues rallied protectively around me. If any doubts about me remained, they were now submerged in the common cause.

A radio commentator named John Madigan added his condemnation three nights later.

The 1975 Oscar . . . Emmy . . . Tony . . . and Grammy awards for bad taste . . . all of them . . . have just been won by Irv Kupcinet of the *Sun-Times*. Nothing can happen in the remainder of the year to top Kup's report of last Friday that a *Chicago Tribune* man is undergoing a sex-change operation.

Kup described the *Trib* staffer as "one of Chicago's top newspapermen" . . . pleaded with the man's "friends and co-workers [to] help him through his ordeal" . . . said he had agreed not to reveal the man's name "because members of his family still are not aware of the change."

This was all camouflage . . . of course. An effort to dress the item with compassion when the purpose of revealing the sex change was to shock. This wasn't something *Sun-Times* readers needed to know. Particularly since they still don't know anything of any substance. All that this report did was to start a lot of gossip and guessing. There's still notoriety and stigma attached to homosexuality and lesbianism and sex change. Maybe there shouldn't be. But there is.

And Kup's presentation of it as a "blind item" succeeded in smearing dozens of *Tribune* men. . . . None of the onus is taken off by Kup explaining why he didn't reveal the name of the man. Sure Kup talked with the man. He would have preferred the item *never* printed. Even in this blind fashion.

And Kup's patronizing attitude to the *Tribune*'s executives and employees! He "trusts" they'll "help" the man. That's a complete fake. Dozens of *Tribune* people have known about the sex change for months and have treated the affair as nothing at all. As nobody's business but the man himself.

If Irv Kupcinet is about to start a sensational

pattern . . . the *Tribune* can suggest some information . . . suppressed for years . . . regarding
people in the Field newspapers. Some of it hitting
very close to Kup.

I wasn't crazy about Madigan's lumping transsexualism
together with homosexuality and lesbianism (probably the
homosexuals and lesbians weren't crazy about it either).
And I felt distinctly offended that a reference to me should
be construed as "smearing dozens of *Tribune* men" (though
the point may have been accurate enough). But I was grateful for his indignation on behalf of me and my friends. And I
was even perversely grateful to Kupcinet, whose column un-
wittingly clinched my acceptance in the newsroom.

Once secure on the copy desk, I allowed myself to complete my drift across the gender line. Some of my progress
came by design, some out of pure absentmindedness. I deliberately began to sign my name as "Nancy" on all my work
and thus conveyed the fact that I no longer wanted to be addressed as a man. My friends did their best to oblige me,
though it took most of them a few months to learn to do it
reflexively. I began to wear earrings in the office, simply because I forgot to take them off one afternoon when I came
to work. I started wearing a bra to the office with malice
aforethought. But the lipstick—like the earrings—came because I forgot to take it off before entering the Tower.

One resolve I made solemnly and irrevocably, and stuck
to for about three months: I would not wear a skirt in the
office until I had undergone surgery. I don't know why I insisted on restraint on this one point, but no matter where I
went in the morning, as the hour for work approached I
dashed home to change from skirt to slacks. Then one after-

noon, having lingered over lunch with a friend and found my bus late and time running out, I abandoned even that last reservation and entered the newsroom in a light-blue linen skirt and white sandals. After everything else they had already suffered with me, the news staff did not blink an eye at my appearance in skirts, nor did they ever say a word to me about it. I understand, however, that they said quite a lot among themselves.

TEN

Although my metamorphosis would inevitably become apparent to my *Tribune* colleagues, it remained unknown to my family in Connecticut, whom I frequently did not see from one year to the next. It seemed necessary that my sisters, at least, should be told about what was happening to me. And so one evening, after I had paid my first visit to the Harry Benjamin people in New York, I took a train up to New Haven. My oldest sister met me at the railroad station, now almost deserted, ill lit, and shabby from disuse. She and I were also showing signs of wear and tear, for that matter, with me forty-seven years old and her going on for sixty, but I was delighted to find her waiting for me at the head of the old concrete ramp. Of my three sisters, I had been closest to her and loved her most, and she had often turned to me in times of trouble, virtually the only times she had. I was with her at her wedding and throughout the week of her divorce trial, and in between I had stood the long vigil of her obstetrical labor and made a dozen tire-screeching rescue missions to her apartment to drag her out of brawls with her husband. As a child, I had often been allowed to tag along when her dates took her swimming or hiking, and it was one of her friends, a Yale undergraduate, who gave me my first airplane ride, in an open Waco biplane. When I became a Yale undergraduate myself, my roommate and I often dined with her. We had shared a lot of secrets, and I thought I had a claim on her affections.

She drove me out to the suburbs, to one of those franchise restaurants that offer an all-you-can-eat salad bar and inedible steaks, and there, with the help of a great deal of burgundy served by the carafe, I told her that I was turning into a woman. I realized almost as soon as the words were out that I had misjudged her badly as a confidante. She was shocked, uncomprehending, and disapproving. (When I got back to Chicago she sent me a newspaper clipping about the male menopause with red-ink marks to underline her conviction that I was unbalanced. In case I missed the point, she also sent me a comic greeting card bearing a funny picture of a squirrel and a joke about being nuts.)

After supper, she drove me out to the white clapboard house and left me with my mother, having first admonished me to say nothing about my delusion. I had not intended to tell my mother—and in fact have not told her as of this writing—but even though I did not allow myself to be overtly feminine, our relationship was altered that weekend. My mother had been working for almost a year on needlecraft projects to be sold at the Christmas church fair. There were potholders and pincushions, aprons and eyeglass cases, toys and traveling cases, some monogrammed, some decorated with rickrack or tiny ship's signal flags, all wrapped in tissue paper. Shyly at first, then with increasing confidence, she brought them forth and laid them out for my inspection on what had once been my youngest sister's bed. I had done enough sewing to appreciate the skill of her execution and the cleverness with which she had conceived or plagiarized her designs. She had put hundreds of hours into this work, and I could see that my praise meant a lot to her.

From the Christmas fair projects we progressed to fabrics, house plants, cooking, decorating, cleaning. For the first time we talked without antagonism but with something approaching respect, even love. I had known her to be courageous and competent, but now she was being affectionate. I could stay with her only a day before flying back to Chicago, but in those hours I caught my first glimpse of what it might have been like if I had been born a daughter instead of the son we both detested.

A few months later, I wrote to my mother's rector, informing him of my condition and asking for his guidance. "As you understand my mother," I wrote, "do you think any remote possibility exists that she could be led to an understanding of transsexualism and to a reconciliation with me as her daughter instead of her son? Would I not do her the greatest kindness by keeping my trap shut and a tweed coat and tie on hand for occasional visits? Would my silence be unconscionably dishonest? Would my declaration be cruelly selfish? What do you think I ought to do?"

The rector wrote back: "In our Christian ethics supposedly we search for truth. On the other hand, your mother is advanced in age, and she derives more comfort from you and your career than you may realize. Even for so-called modern liberals, your proposed action is a rare and startling event. For a lady like your mother, it would be like an earthquake. . . ."

He was mistaken about the comfort my mother derived from my career. Her generation had been brought up to consider newspaper work not quite respectable, except perhaps on the *Times* of either New York or London. She had never even pretended interest in my writing, and I had stopped telling her about it years ago. We had always approached each other warily if at all. From my childhood we had seldom touched or kissed; it was considered vulgar to display emotion, except for anger, jealousy, and spitefulness. I had learned early to confide no secret and reveal no weakness, for my mother would exploit it to my disadvantage. Yet some deep instinct urged me to confide this most dreadful secret. I felt certain that once the shock had passed, we would have the loving bond that had eluded us all those years. But it has been the unanimous opinion of the rector, of Ellen, and of my two oldest sisters that the shock would never pass, that it might indeed kill her.

For my mother is ill now, unable to drive a car, not even trusted to handle her own checkbook. Because she reads and writes with great difficulty, we communicate by telephone, and in those conversations we have finally achieved a greater closeness than we ever knew before. We giggle and gossip and commiserate, sometimes for half an hour at a time, which in my family is sinfully long for a long-distance call. Often she laments that we cannot be together for these chats, but she does not press the point. She hears my woman's voice and shares my woman's concerns, and I think she is glad to leave it at that.

Perhaps I should long ago have throttled this instinct to attach myself to my family. We are none of us very nice people, neither loving nor loyal nor even polite to each other. In those hours when we have gathered in the library for cocktails at Christmastime or Thanksgiving, we have routinely said the most dreadful, unpardonable things to each other.

My youngest sister alone has had the good sense to oppose these proceedings; she either doesn't attend them or she storms out of the house before it's time to do the dishes, slamming the door thunderously behind her. She has devoted her life to waging guerrilla warfare against conventional society, so when I became hell-bent to enlist the sympathies of some member of the family I was especially tempted to confide in her. But she has also, as long as I've known her, been a compulsive stool pigeon. Ever since she mastered human speech, she has used it to snitch on somebody, usually me, and I learned in infancy that any secret I was dumb enough to tell her would be passed on to my mother within an hour. So if I wanted to keep my mother in the dark, I knew better than to enlighten my youngest sister.

That left my middle sister, a woman of impeccable character and the highest standards. I cannot think what madness drove me to probe for some tender spot in her stony heart, but I gave it my best try. A few days before Christmas, I wrote her one of my wordy letters, setting forth the whole matter of my gender disorder. "I don't know how to put this well," I began, "so I'll put it badly and throw myself on the mercy of the court."

It took me three single-spaced pages and four days of composition to state my case.

"All of the above seems rather afield from the joyous Christmas season," I wrote at the end. "And it is a joyous season for me despite the sadness that accompanies profound change. It's easy enough to compile a list of regrets. I'm sorry that I could not live up to everyone's expectations. But most of all, I'm grateful for four days off at Christmas,

for friends who accept me, for our plastic Christmas tree
with its Italian lights, for heat in the radiators, for a good
book to finish. Life kicks us around some, but it has treated
me fairly well, on balance. I hope it treats you well too. And
I hope you can forgive your brother's failure and accept me
as a devoted sister. (Just what you needed—another sister!)
Anyway, I think of you both lovingly."

I signed the letter "Nancy."

My sister's reply, when it came two weeks later, was a
model of concision. Consisting of two lined notebook pages,
it was packed mostly with such phrases as "Your 'informa-
tive' letter has confused me . . ." and "I really don't understand . . ." and "I really find your news hard to understand, and hope you'll give your situation further thought
before taking irrevocable steps. . . ." (It was then a month
before my surgery.)

But I hadn't really had to open her letter to know that I
had struck out. She had addressed it to "Mr." and had used
my old, by now discarded name.

We exchanged a few more salvos of correspondence, but
neither side scored a hit. In my last effort, I wrote: "I have
wondered if I could come East and see you both, if only for
a few hours, to try to demonstrate that I am not a freak or
an ogre, that I am still the same person underneath. It might
help you to understand if we could talk about it a little. I do
value and love you both, and despite the happiness I have
recently learned to derive from friendship, life somehow
seems terribly bleak without a family of one's own. It's only
a half-formed idea, but let me know if you think it might
work out."

That letter went unanswered, which is answer enough.
Later, when my mother was seriously stricken and in the

hospital for weeks, my sisters elected not to tell me lest I come flouncing East in drag and scare the poor lady to death. When eventually I learned about it through an aunt, I telephoned my middle sister to ask if I could please take her out to dinner and talk about my mother. She refused to see me.

I have heard about transsexuals who were welcomed by their families, but I believe rejection to be the more common experience. It has certainly been mine.

But while the family, from whom a measure of loyalty is traditionally expected, was casting me to the dogs, my friends on the *Tribune* were drawing closer. I had never had much talent for friendship as a man; even as I craved it, I would rebuff it when it was offered. I was just too awkward to play the games of human relationships. But now as a woman I was slipping into the intermediate class and winning a few matches.

It was for this—for the social role of woman—that I had longed to change my gender, more than from a compulsion to swathe myself in lingerie or spread my legs to men. And it is this even now that most makes me feel like a woman: to be among people. At home, in the solitude of my apartment, my gender recedes. I slip into a moth-eaten woolen bathrobe, left over from my man's life, because it is warm. I don't bother with makeup or earrings—who's to see me, after all? But I remain a woman: I shave my legs or wash my hair, and beneath my moth-eaten bathrobe I wear bra and panties or a nightgown. Yet these things no longer hold the significance they once did; they are now merely a condition of my life, like always drinking orange juice for breakfast or reading the Sunday comics from the back to the front.

It is when I lock my door behind me and set forth into the

world that I feel myself truly to be a woman. My spine straightens, my shoulders draw back, my head is held high, and I walk with pride. I feel wonderfully happy and strong —strong enough to trust myself to others, strong enough to rely on their love in return. And they seldom disappoint me.

It was not that way in the beginning. I had known almost from the moment I first put on the green sailor dress that as a woman I would need friends even more than as a man. But how I was to make these friends I could not imagine, and so I wrote to Jan Morris in England, asking if we could correspond about these problems. In turning me down ("if I embarked upon a correspondence with everyone who wants me to I would never get another book written"), Miss Morris added: "I think you'd do much better to confide in some of your ordinary friends, whom you well may find, if my own experience is anything to go by, much more understanding than you expect."

I had never thought of confiding in some of my ordinary friends. I asked Ellen's advice, as I did in all weighty matters, and between us we chose a friend on whom to try it out, an editor on the *Sunday Magazine* with whom I had a close bond of mutual respect. Lustily relaxed in his masculinity, he seemed a person who should not feel threatened by my confession. And he had left his wife and children to live with another woman, a fact that argued for his liberality. By chance, he invited me down for a drink a few nights later, and I made up my mind to tell him.

We were talking about the increasing numeralization of life, and I remarked: "Even though we resist the trend, we can't help but memorize a thousand numbers about ourselves. I still know the telephone number we had in New Haven thirty-five years ago and the combination of my bicy-

169

cle padlock. I remember my Social Security number and my Army serial number and the number on the M-1 rifle I had in the infantry. I know I wear a size twelve dress and thirty-six-A bra and size six panties."

If he hadn't already been sitting, I think he would have dropped as if he'd been poleaxed. For an instant his face froze, his hand stuck in midmotion, as though a movie projector had jammed, leaving a single frame immobilized on the screen. Just as quickly he recovered, finished raising his glass to his lips, and began to ask the right questions. And I told him everything—or as much as I knew at the time, which wasn't a great deal. I had not yet gone far on the road to womanhood.

A few nights later, he and his girl came up for drinks at our place. I was wearing a plaid skirt, a long-sleeved brown knit top with mock turtleneck, brown pumps, and a short, blond wig. She was chatty, graceful, amusing. He was tongue-tied. She said I had nice legs. He said almost nothing.

After that night, I didn't hear a word from either of them for more than a year. But then word of his anguish reached me through friends: He was stricken, he knew that I had counted on him, and he was overwhelmed by guilt. But he "just couldn't handle this." It was a phrase I was to hear frequently in the coming years, and one that I never fully understood. I had thought I was the one who had to handle this—I and possibly Ellen. What I could not grasp was the fact that my joy was their sorrow. I exulted in my emerging gender; they thought it was disgusting. I felt born anew; they thought of me as dead.

In the *Tribune* newsroom, those who just couldn't handle this were obliged to remain a silent minority. They were mostly men of my own age or older, welded for years into the armor of masculinity. My allies were mostly younger women, there being almost no older women on the *Tribune* news staff (or for that matter on most other big metropolitan dailies; on the *Tribune*'s editorial seniority list, I am the highest-ranking woman).

So the men, who still constitute a majority in the newsroom, were at first embarrassed, full of questions that they dared not ask me, uncertain even how to address me. Many of their questions they relayed through Pete, who, in turn, kept me informed of their sentiments toward me (largely favorable, he said) and of the wave of gossip that washed through the newspaper bars. As I began to sign my new name, the slot man for whom I worked started to call me "Nancy" and to correct those who failed to. Everyone had a hard time remembering to call me by my new name and to refer to me in the feminine pronoun. I helped them by nagging every time they erred.

It was in the newspaper bar across Michigan Avenue that my new social relationships—having been well-watered in the newsroom—began to flower. Relaxed and a little bit high, the guys started to treat me like a lady, not only by ordering my drinks and lighting my cigarettes, but also in their attitude toward me, which subtly shifted from comradeship to gentle consideration tinged with superiority. I have always enjoyed the company of men, even during those dark years when I felt myself to be a misfit among them. They are, as an admittedly too broad generality, funnier, bawdier, more direct, and possibly better informed than women. There is also about them a vulnerability, made more poignant by their efforts to conceal it behind their toughness. For challenge and laughter and excitement, for strength and the comfort of arms to hold me, give me a man every time. For confidences, for a little ruthless gossip and defamation of character, for confessions of weakness and a chance to let down one's guard, I'd rather be with women. These may be gender stereotypes, but having played both sides of the street, I can only affirm their validity.

It was also in that newspaper bar that I finally dented the defenses of the *Tribune*'s private Marine Corps. This was a small band of ex-Marines congregated on the telegraph desk of the newsroom. Rather than welcome me as a woman, they had eyed me with mute distaste, like a pack of hounds bristling at the sight of a cat. The Marine Corps makes a religion of manliness, and of all the telegraph-desk Marines, the toughest and manliest was Daugherty—massive and battered, loud and profane, the archetypical gunnery sergeant. Daugherty also worked as a bartender across the street in his spare time, and he was thus occupied one night, wordlessly producing another beer for me each time I finished the last.

"Let me buy you a drink, Nancy," said a friend who had just come by. "What are you having?"

I looked up at Daugherty, towering mountainously before me, his beefy face expressionless. I didn't want to antagonize him by changing my order after he had taken the trouble to remember the brand of beer I was drinking that night. On the other hand, I was saturated with beer and really wanted a bourbon.

"Is it all right if I switch?" I asked him.

Daugherty looked at me in consternation for a moment, then threw back his gigantic head and laughed until the bottles rattled. "I guess you already have," he gasped finally, and from that night, no man ever treated me with greater tenderness or gallantry.

172

Most of these adjustments occurred during the summer and fall before my surgery and were entirely psychological. I had no physical life as a woman, in part because I lacked the anatomical equipment but also because, despite my skirts and lipstick, my friends knew well enough that these blossoms of femininity were grafted onto a male oak. Men willingly took me to supper and opened car doors for me, and they even flirted with me up to a point, but they were motivated largely by the novelty of my situation. When in time we all grew accustomed to the fact that I was a woman, the allure diminished and so did their attentions. I seldom go to the bar across the street anymore, and the men at the paper rarely invite me. Fifty-year-old women don't get invited out a great deal. Even at the height of my belated debutante season, the men who knew my past did not dance with me or kiss me good-night. They would have felt their virility compromised. Most of them still feel that way.

Sexually I remained as innocent as a novice in a nunnery, a condition that was to trouble me more and more when at last I made my appointment with the surgeon. Despite my emotional compulsion, I could not rationally justify the operation. I was comfortable and happy as a woman, and people liked me as a woman. I had this already in hand. Why the surgery? Why acquire a vagina? Merely to complete the trappings of femininity as a sort of transcendent cosmetic? That didn't seem good enough somehow. A vagina, bought at such cost in pain and money, should serve some purpose, and surely that purpose must be sexual. But what if I didn't like sex as a woman? How was I to know?

A few days after Christmas, just six weeks before my operation, I found out.

I was in the bar across the street from Tribune Tower late

one evening, unwinding from the tedium and stress of the newsroom, when I was picked up by a *Tribune* employee named Tony, a man loaded with machismo. I had passed him a thousand times in the Tower lobby with neither of us saying more than "hello," but now he bought me a beer and proceeded to unburden himself.

He had been watching my transition for the last couple of years, he confided, and he had to say that he admired my—if I would pardon the expression—balls (actually he used the Italian word and then translated). He had seen me coming downstairs from the fourth floor to use the public ladies' room on the first floor, and he didn't think it was right that I should have to do that. He thought I had "real class," an opinion he was to offer several times during the evening. (Somehow, I have turned out to be the sort of broad who gets picked up in bars, and often the man doing the picking up will assure me that I have "real class," after which he will suggest the most déclassé way imaginable of spending the night.)

Tony offered to take me home in a cab, and because buses run infrequently on Michigan Avenue at that hour of the night, I accepted. I put on my coat, and Tony excused himself to go to the men's room. "Stand right there," he commanded. It was such a typically male instruction that I laughed, but I did as I was told. While I waited, the news editor left his stool on the far side of the bar to come around to me and take my hand. "I'm going on vacation, so I won't be seeing you for a week," he said, "but I wanted to wish you a happy New Year and good luck." I stood there holding his hand and smiling at him like a high school girl with a crush on her math teacher. I was beginning to feel quite pleasant.

In the taxi racing north on Lake Shore Drive, Tony began to make his moves. Which variety of apparatus did I prefer, he wanted to know: his own (gesturing toward the tightly stretched crotch of his trousers) or "the other," indicating the same general area of my own body and quite forgetting that I was anatomically endowed exactly as he was, if not to the same degree. I replied tremulously that I didn't know, never having had an opportunity to make a comparison.

Tony pulled me to him masterfully and began kissing me and trying to unbutton my coat. It was a double-breasted coat, fastened at the neck and belted at the waist, with five buttons from top to bottom, all of which worked stiffly, the fabric being a sturdy wool and almost new. When he had penetrated this, he encountered a still more obdurate barrier: a ribbed turtleneck top, the neck of which I had additionally secured with a tightly knotted scarf. By now the taxi had turned off Lake Shore Drive (somewhat perilously, with the driver dividing his attention between road and rearview mirror), and Tony's time was running out. He was becoming agitated, and so was I. When I saw that he wasn't going to make it without some help, I guided his hand under the bottom of my turtleneck, and he contrived to wriggle it over the top of my slip and inside my bra. So far, so good. Then, predictably, his other hand embarked on a probing movement upward beneath my skirt.

Mercifully, the taxi now drew up in front of my apartment building, and Tony was obliged to disengage for a moment.

He would come upstairs with me, he panted.

Out of the question, I answered. It was a very small apartment, and my roommate would be there. (I no longer used the word "wife" in referring to Ellen.)

He would be "discreet," he promised.

The possibility of Tony being discreet was at that point something that I could not easily imagine. "The living room lights are on," I protested. "My roommate is still up. This just isn't going to work." (The household arrangements weren't the only thing that wasn't going to work, I thought balefully. What on earth did he expect to do to me?)

Tony told the taxi driver to wait and slipped him some money to make sure that he did. Then he escorted me upstairs, where, as I had predicted, Ellen was not only awake but fully clothed and happy to see me. She did not at first see Tony, breathing hard in the doorway behind me, but as soon as she did, she tactfully withdrew into the bedroom, leaving me to deal with events as best I could.

Tony drew me roughly out onto the landing, pulled off my coat and flung it across the banister. Then with one hand he clasped me to him while with the other he unzipped his fly and lowered his trousers far enough to present a potent omen of his intentions, but not so far as to impede his progress should circumstances suggest a hasty retreat.

Despite our precarious situation, I was beginning to enjoy the proceedings, so I did what little I could for Tony, which was a good deal more than I had ever supposed I would do for a man. Somehow that failed to bring him relief. Tony then proposed to assault me from the rear, but a decent respect for convention prompted me to decline. It was only with great difficulty, however, that I dissuaded him. At length, reluctantly, like a disappointed little boy, Tony zipped up his pants and descended to his waiting taxi. I went inside to bed, elated. I was still terribly excited, but I was also triumphant and relieved. I had liked it. Liked it? Hell, I had loved it! It was going to be all right! My sexual orientation conformed with my gender, or at least was askew in the same direction. Now I knew what I was going to do with my new vagina, and given half a chance, I was going to do it often.

But for now, I could find no physical release. After a year of massive doses by syringe and pill, the estrogens had made me impotent as a male, a result sometimes called "chemical castration." For the last six months, Ellen and I had lived together truly as sisters, though less and less as friends. We quarreled incessantly.

Dr. Pomeroy, the psychologist, had predicted this when we had gone to see him together the previous spring, two months before the unpleasantness of our European tour.

"I shall sit over there," Pomeroy had said, establishing at the outset that this would be a well-structured interview, "and you two may sit here and here."

I suspected that this was a sort of test, that he would find significance in where each of us chose to sit, but as a manipulator of interviews myself, I rebelled against following his stage directions. "I'm sorry," I said, "I'm afraid I wasn't paying attention. Could you repeat the rules of the game?"

But Ellen had already taken the more comfortable of the two seats, and the validity of the experiment was compromised.

Pomeroy, I soon perceived, was a superb interviewer, far better than I. The interview lasted precisely fifty minutes, at the end of which he said: "I will not attempt to tell you now whether you are a candidate for sex-reassignment surgery. But I will tell you both this: If you continue on your present course, I don't think your marriage will last another three years."

I didn't believe him. I was dressed as a man that day in

gray flannels and sport coat, feeling rather like a woman but very much like a husband. Ellen and I had never been closer. No matter what I might be now or become later, we would always have each other. Pomeroy must be mistaken.

"That is a very smart man," Ellen said when we had left him. "He knows a lot."

I did not think so at the time, but I recalled his words in Paris as Ellen and I tramped sullenly through the Louvre. Our marriage would not last three years? My God, three months later, for all practical purposes it was dead!

ELEVEN

I still have to return to my electrologist every couple of months to eradicate the stray facial hairs that occasionally crop out, not like whiskers now but wisps. It reminds me of going back to school when I enter the old electrolysis parlor, with its reclining dentist's chair and the electric box that powers the needle. I remember my weekly ordeals there as one might recall the suffering of written examinations—proudly and almost affectionately. Then I settle back in the chair and feel the needle's sting as Helena tells me the latest transsexual gossip.

Almost every transsexual in Chicago has come to Helena at one time or another, as have gays, transvestites, female impersonators, straight males, and biological women. Helena mothers them all. She is a short, plump woman with an odd, squeaky voice, a vast acquaintance with wickedness, and a childlike, self-protective innocence, and she has a word of advice for everyone. Some she advises on finances, and I have known her to escort clients into the nearby savings and loan to open accounts. Others she guides in the selection of makeup or clothes. She recommends doctors to administer hormones and visits her clients at Cook County Hospital after their sex-reassignment surgery. She knows what nightclubs they work in and whom they're living with and whether their boyfriends treat them well or badly. She is invariably invited to the annual transvestite ball, which is always held in one of the city's best hotels. She knows where to get breast implants and where not to. She can find a dressmaker to alter a man's skirts. She keeps track of all the transvestite clubs and their meetings.

I am exceedingly fond of Helena, though I have availed myself of none of her services beyond her needle. At first, I didn't even tell her why I was having my beard removed. She could scarcely conceal her curiosity. She would dart in with little questions about my sexual views, then hastily retreat, embarrassed by her impertinence. Once a week I showed up at exactly 5:30 P.M. with my crew cut and my tweed sport coat—I was so straight! At length, Helena concluded that I was uprooting my beard out of a compulsion for cleanliness. "That's it, isn't it?" she asked in sympathetic tones. "You just want to look clean." That first Christmas, I dropped in on her wearing a wig, dress, and makeup, and bearing a gift-wrapped box. She didn't recognize me. I said I was leaving a present for my brother, and at the next appointment Helena told me how delighted she had been to meet my sister.

When at last I revealed my transsexualism, no one was happier or more relieved than Helena. She had been afraid that I was indeed straight. But she continued to fret about me, suggesting that I might like to meet various people or join certain clubs that could help me. Perhaps I would have had an easier time if I had accepted her offers, but I didn't want to associate with other transsexuals. Aside from Ellen, I had no guide and wanted none. I would do this thing alone.

Inevitably I reached a point where I had to acknowledge my need for specialized help, for some authority with whom I could discuss the strange things that were happening to me and who could tell me when I might be ready to face the scalpel. I never doubted now that I would be .eady one day; I just wanted to make sure that I didn't jump the gun. In a matter as important as changing one's sex, it seemed necessary to proceed cautiously.

But finding help for transsexuals isn't an easy, straightforward search like trying to find a periodontist to fix your decaying gums or a dermatologist to cure your acne. Given any of humanity's ordinary afflictions—cancer, gonorrhea, peptic ulcers—you can invariably find a physician eager to heal your lesion and take your money, but a transsexual occupies a far different position. Whereas the entire medical profession is eager for a shot at your tumor, fracture or psychosis, it wants no part of the transsexual's gender confusion. The male transsexual comes as a supplicant. Few doctors will treat him—or are equipped to. Few psychiatrists understand his disorder and none can cure it. Few surgeons can grant his prayer and those that can are expensive. Even estrogens—his most fundamental need—can be legally obtained only by prescription, and most doctors will refuse to write that prescription. In desperation, some transsexuals resort to swallowing their wives' birth-control pills, an expedient that works inadequately and very slowly. Others turn to a sort of black market that operates within the homosexual community, paying exorbitant sums for Premarin or diethylstilbestrol like junkies buying heroin. Indeed, the drug addict will find more sympathy, more doctors willing to treat him, more social agencies established to help him, than will the transsexual seeking release from his torment.

The magazine *New Times* recently estimated that "there are twenty-odd gender identity clinics in the U.S. and twenty hospitals where surgery is regularly performed," probably as good a guess as any. There are also sex-change mills in foreign cities such as Tijuana and Tokyo, the most famous of which is the one maintained in Casablanca by Dr. Georges Burou, the mysterious "Dr. B——" who operated on Jan Morris.

As a rule, American surgeons demand a psychiatric recommendation as a ticket of admission to the operating room, not so much out of concern for the transsexual patient as to protect their own skins. Their position with respect to malpractice insurance is tenuous, and because the medical establishment takes a dim view of sex-reassignment surgery, they operate always under the threat of professional disapproval. If a case were to blow up on them—if, for instance, a postsurgical patient were to commit suicide, as happens, or worse still were to sue for damages—they might sustain heavy financial loss or even forfeit their licenses.

Another grave peril in the minds of most surgeons is that they won't be paid. It's a justifiable fear, for a good many transsexuals are deadbeats, and surgery performed even in a passably equipped hospital is expensive. (A recent bill for my own surgery at the University of Virginia hospital—by no means the most expensive in the country—included these charges:

> Private room per day......................$102.00
> Operating room............................... 520.00

Recovery room.................................. 30.00
Anesthesia supplies.......................... 130.00

This particular bill, which covered a hospital stay of fifteen days, ran on through thirty-nine such items totaling $2,153.80 and still didn't include the surgeon's $500 fee. And that was for my second stretch at the University of Virginia, a patch-up job. The first, which lasted twenty-nine days and required three trips to the operating room, cost much more. Surgeons' fees that time were $2,000, again not notably high in comparison with the going rate for this work.)

Routinely, then, surgeons demand cash on the barrelhead when asked to operate on transsexuals. In consequence, many transsexuals work as male prostitutes to save the necessary cash, and are then often defrauded of their nest eggs by their boyfriends and pimps, or robbed by the "fruit-hustlers" who prey on homosexuals. Although skilled male prostitutes in Chicago can earn as much as one hundred dollars a trick, their losses and expenses may keep them at their trade for years before they can accumulate enough money to pay their surgeons and ransom themselves from bondage. After their operations, many continue in prostitution, it being by then the only way of life they know. The rest take up less demanding work (beautician is a favorite profession) or settle down with husbands who may never guess their wives' anatomical secret. (Even gynecologists are sometimes fooled by a skillful job. Some of Edgerton's alumnae have passed the physical exams necessary to enlist in the women's military services, though heaven knows why they would want to.)

Any and all of these hurdles can be surmounted through a

gray homosexual underground. I have heard of one psychiatrist who will write the required recommendation for fifty dollars—no questions asked. And somewhere, in some flea-bitten, ill-equipped hospital, there is always a doctor—not necessarily a board-certified surgeon—who will lop off the despised organ for a fee, payable in advance.

For myself, I had saved the money, though as it happened the *Tribune*'s medical insurance paid my bills. But I stubbornly resisted the course that lay through the underground. I was a transsexual, but I wasn't a criminal, and I could see no reason why I should slink furtively into the operating room. And so, in March 1974, I wrote to Harry Benjamin, the most prominent and respected physician in the field, asking if he could recommend a specialist in Chicago or, failing that, treat me himself.

"Unfortunately," he replied, "there is at the moment nobody in Chicago to whom I could refer you with good conscience. . . ."

Thus that November, I made my first pilgrimage to the Harry Benjamin shrine in New York and was granted what proved to be my only audience with the saint himself. The hallowed ground was a suite of ratty offices on Seventy-fourth Street just off Park Avenue, and I entered with that solemn sensation of taking yet another irrevocable step. I wore a Brooks Brothers tweed sport coat, gray flannels, and a button-down shirt, a costume chosen to demonstrate humility about my aspirations to womanhood. Beneath my armor of tweed, however, my bosom swelled with pride and estrogens.

The blessings conferred by the Benjamin establishment were largely spiritual, for there was little they could do for me physically. I was examined by an associate of Benjamin's, a young internist named Charles Ihlenfeld, who listened raptly as I recited a string of anecdotes about Vietnam, the newspaper business, and the torrid dance floor at Alfie's. Whether these convinced him that I was a suitable candidate for sex-reassignment surgery he declined to say. He told me to return the next spring and at that time to see their consulting psychologist, Wardell B. Pomeroy. Despite the lack of a specific diagnosis, I felt relieved to have unburdened myself, as I might have felt after praying at Lourdes. Other sanctuaries now ministered to transsexuals—some were larger, some perhaps superior in medical science—but I had gone to the mount and had sat at the feet of the prophet. I took a snobbish satisfaction from that.

There were, I eventually discovered, at least two gender-identity clinics in Chicago, and I took a stab at getting into both of them. Like most others that I have since looked into, they operated on the premise that they were the master who held the treat and I was the dog and had better roll over on command or I wasn't going to get it.

Cook County Hospital's program cost less than most but required as a condition of admission that I attend group therapy sessions every Thursday morning at which candidates exchanged girlish confidences about their gender problems. Many gender clinics demand submission to group therapy. When I protested that I had to be in my office on Thursday mornings, they implied that that was my tough luck. The inference was that you may want to be a woman, kiddo, but there's something wrong with you if you want to be the kind of woman who holds down a job and gets to work on time and does all the other things that millions of other American women do; if you want to be a woman, you have to make a full-time profession of it. Besides, they told me sternly, they had a very long waiting list. I asked them to add my name to the list and let me know when my turn came up, and they said they would, but I never heard from them again. That's a pity, too, because I later met some of the people who staff the Cook County gender program and found them knowledgeable and sympathetic. And their surgeon, Bangalore Jayaram, may be the best in the country, despite the gargantuan public hospital in which he usually works. He frequently is called upon to repair sex-reassignment surgery that has been botched at other hospitals, as indeed he eventually repaired mine. It was my fourth operation, and he achieved a superb result. I wished I had gone to him in the first place.

The other gender-identity program was operated by Northwestern Memorial Hospital, one of the city's most august institutions. Even then, in February 1975, Northwestern's gender people were keeping a low profile, as if they were engaged in a disreputable occupation like peddling bootleg whiskey. To my dismay, they required that one begin with their lawyer "since it is a fairly complex legal problem," as they wrote me. (I never found it a complex legal problem, though it may be for the doctors.) Reluctantly, I did go around to see their lawyer, and what he wanted was $600 payable in advance. For that $600 the customer was promised a series of aptitude tests and an interview with a psychologist, all of which, I was assured, could be scheduled in a single eight-hour day. They would then undertake to tell me whether I was a transsexual or merely an imitation of one. No surgery, no shots, no help—just tests. When I protested that 600 bucks seemed like a lot for one day's tests, I again encountered the that's-your-tough-luck-buddy syndrome that characterizes so many in this field. I decided to keep my money and take my chances elsewhere.

I was then working as a financial reporter and maintaining my male façade in the office, though on weekends and vacations I was living as a woman. My transition was gaining momentum but there was yet no sense of urgency. I believed I had time to do the thing calmly, deliberately, and with as much prudence as one can bring to changing one's sex.

Within the next eight months, I nearly lost my job, my secret became known in Tribune Tower, and I was working in the newsroom as a woman. I was afloat on a cloud of euphoria, but I was also beset with rising emotional problems. Ellen and I had gone through the fire of our European tour and I was facing the bleakness of paradise lost, and for this awful price I had exacted from us both I had received one jewel: I was nine-tenths of a woman. Just one physical anomaly remained to set me apart from my sisters. But what a crucial anomaly! Until it could be excised, I was exposed to a hundred social perils and denied a hundred human rights. I might conceal it with clothing and shrink it with hormones, yet it was always with me—an absurd object of no importance, except that the world and the law would always judge me by it. No matter that I then lacked the impulse to make love to a man. I might as well have it off and solve all my problems with a few quick cuts of the knife. I wasn't eager to face the surgeon, but now I was at least resigned.

And so on our return from Europe, I set about the search. I had given up on the two recognized gender clinics in Chicago, but I knew a couple of names and could discover others. The Harry Benjamin people had a favored surgeon in New York, and I would see him. An acquaintance at Helena's electrolysis parlor swore by a man out West, and I would write to him. My own plastic surgeon—who occasionally dug a troublesome wart out of my hide but didn't do sex changes himself—suggested two others: a man at

Johns Hopkins and Milton Edgerton at the University of Virginia. I wrote to both of them. And perhaps the most authoritative list came from the Erickson Educational Foundation (now defunct), which sent me four names, again including Edgerton's, of whom I wrote to three.

The replies were a mixed bag. Most were heavily bureaucratic in their syntax ("at the time of the initial appointment, all pertinent issues will be discussed . . ." "As per your letter asking for information regarding the requirements . . ." "I will forward your letter to S—— who can give the appropriate information about our screening . . ."). Several emphasized the need to get the money up front ("we must unfortunately have payment in advance . . ." "we and the hospital must receive cash at the time the surgery is done . . .").

The funniest answer came from the man out West, whose form letter read like an F.A.O. Schwarz toy catalogue: $1,000 for genital surgery, $500 for breast implants, $400 for a nose bob, $250 for a "tracheal shave" (a reduction of the Adam's apple, required by many transsexuals though happily not by me). I studied the list in amazement. Gosh! He could make me look like Shirley Temple, even if he had to ship me home in a box. My curiosity whetted, I wrote and asked him about his qualifications to perform such miracles, wondering if he was a board-certified surgeon. He replied: "In the five (5) years we have probably done more than anyone else in the United States and the results have been quite good. Thank you." Scratch one candidate. (I later was told that, while his cosmetic results were simply awful, he did produce a vagina that performed just beautifully in bed.)

Implicit in most of the letters was an overriding allegiance to their own systems and the unspoken warning that any deviation would spell my doom. (I have since heard behavioral scientists at a symposium on transsexualism fervently describe the rigid requirements of the programs—seventeen rigid requirements in one case. And if the candidate slipped up on a requirement, said one of these experts exultantly, "we exclude him from the program!")

"The sex-reassignment program," the Cleveland Clinic wrote, "includes a psychiatric evaluation, psychological testing, endocrinologic evaluation and treatment, and transsexual surgery where indicated. Except under very rare circumstances, the evaluation takes a minimum of six to nine months with regular psychotherapy sessions." Never mind that it would be impossible for me to attend regular sessions of anything in Cleveland, 343 miles from Chicago, or the fact that I had already had thorough endocrinologic evaluation and treatment. If I wanted to get into their operating room, I had to run their obstacle course.

The single oasis of humanity and reason in this desert of dogma lay in Edgerton's letter.

> We prefer at Virginia to use the two-stage inversion method for surgical construction of the vagina and labia in the male transsexual patient [he wrote, getting down to essentials in the second paragraph]. It is an improved method that we believe gives the ideal softness and quality to the lining of the reconstructed vagina. We have had a high percentage of success with this method and consider it to be the most effective procedure we have to produce satisfactory female genitalia.

I didn't detect one note of advocacy in Edgerton's words, though much later I learned that his two-stage procedure was almost unique.

189

Two separate surgical procedures are required to change the male to a female, and the professional fees for these operations are $1,000 apiece. In addition to the professional fees for the surgery, you can expect to pay hospitalization and psychiatric consultation fees which vary, but in general hospitalization runs around $125 a day. . . .

Approximately twelve days of hospital care are required for the initial step and approximately four days are required two weeks later. The two-week waiting period between stages allows the blood supply to improve so that the labia and a small clitoris may be constructed in the second stage.

The first step for a transsexual patient involves coming to Charlottesville for a three–four-day evaluation which involves psychiatric interviews, psychological tests, and examination by a plastic surgeon, gynecologist, and a urologist. The cost for this is approximately $300. Usually, if the initial evaluation shows that a candidate is suitable for surgery, a period of five months must transpire before any physical treatment or social change is attempted.

If after you have digested all this information, you still feel motivated to pursue surgery, I hope you will contact us and come to Charlottesville for the initial workup. Your letter suggests that your sense of humor remains undaunted, and that is an admirable quality. I do look forward to meeting you.

I liked him right off. He conceded that the relationship between surgeon and patient was two-way, that I must be sold on him just as he must be sold on me. None of the others had suggested such courtesy. He didn't insist that I come to him on my knees with my money in hand. Though I couldn't judge his professional skill, I looked him up in the physicians directory in the *Tribune* morgue and found his credentials to be first-class. Still, to give myself a choice, I flew to New York in November 1975 to see the surgeon preferred by the Harry Benjamin people. I did not prefer him myself. He had an office in a shabby neighborhood better suited to an abortion mill. His receptionist was rude, his waiting room crowded, his supply of magazines inadequate. He kept me waiting for an hour and a half while patients who had arrived after me went in before. By the time I was ushered into his sanctum I was hungry, crabby, and ready to go home. The last flight of the day was leaving for Chicago in forty minutes, and I meant to be on it whether this guy was willing to operate on me or not.

The interview got off to a bad start. He had mislaid my file, including the vital psychiatric recommendation from Pomeroy, and had no recollection of my letters, on which I had spent a good deal of time. One of the first male chauvinist pigs I had encountered as a woman, he refused to divulge any details of his surgical technique or even to name the private hospital in which he proposed to operate on me. He stood me on a little metal stool, told me to lift my skirt and drop my panties, and seized me with a paper towel. It was by now too small, he said scornfully, there wasn't enough tissue left; he would have to take a skin graft from my leg. Would it leave a scar? I asked. He shrugged as if it was a stupid question and said he didn't know. At last, grudgingly, he said he would operate on me in two months. Not if I can help it, buster! I snarled to myself, and ran from his office. I had just twelve minutes to catch my plane.

"Just a minute," called the disagreeable receptionist. "That will be fifty dollars." Frantically I scribbled a check, raced for a taxi, and reached my plane seconds before they closed the door.

I flew down to Charlottesville a month later to meet Edgerton and his associates. I have made the same trip half a dozen times since, sometimes joyful, sometimes scared, but always hopeful.

My first appointment came late in the afternoon, and having arrived early I whiled away some of the time in conversation with the nurses and secretaries, all of whom were willing to pause and trade jokes or to show me where I could sneak a cigarette. Edgerton's courtesy, I decided, must rub off on the whole staff. Presently they put me in an examining room, and in a few minutes Marsh knocked and entered.

"And why have you come to us?" he asked after we had chatted for a few minutes.

"To try to con you into performing sex-reassignment surgery on me."

Marsh didn't falter but merely asked, "And what is your genetic sex?"

I was thrown, but I was also elated that he didn't know I was a genetic male. Many months later in the hospital snack bar, Marsh explained his uncertainty. My file had been switched with another, and as a result, when he walked in on me, he was under the impression that he was meeting some middle-aged woman in search of a face-lift. Most gender-identity clinics depend on elaborate psychological evaluations and testing, but as Edgerton later told me, the ultimate decision at his clinic rests on a gut reaction to the question: Is this person truly a man or a woman? With

Marsh, at least, I had passed that test in the first three minutes.

Before I left that evening, I was sent to the medical art department and photographed twice in color, once dressed and once naked. ("That naked one just about blew my mind," Edgerton's assistant, Marcy Rankins, told me later. She had known me only as a woman.) I had been interviewed by Edgerton and Futrell as well as Marsh—Edgerton quiet but filling the room with his presence; Futrell boyish, earnest, and with blood on his shoes. And all three had examined me, stripped and draped and in lithotomy while they peered and poked, their voices rising from behind the sheet where I couldn't see them. "You see this, Jeff? We've got about thirty-five centimeters. . . ."

The next day I was examined by the urologist and the day after that by the gynecologist, an enchanting man named Ulysses (Jim) Turner, who didn't poke my anatomy at all but merely chatted for an hour. The next summer he would tell me that, like Edgerton, he had been weighing a "gut reaction" toward me as a woman. "For instance," he said, "ninety-nine out of one hundred women will sit in that chair exactly the way you do—and not one man."

The observation startled me. Certainly as a man I had made an effort to sit in a manly way with legs spraddled or ankle cocked on knee, but I had never given the matter much thought as a woman. Now I froze myself to determine precisely what it was about my sitting that had caught Turner's notice: ankles crossed, knees demurely together and turned slightly sideways to him, hands clasped in my lap. Yes, come to think of it, that was exactly how any woman would sit in formal confrontation (though she wouldn't sit that way at home, and neither would I). And I had adopted that position instinctively, the only way I could since I have no talent for mimicry. It was an instinct Ellen had noticed. "You were sitting just like a woman," she complained once after a lecture I had attended as a man.

I had to make one more call before flying back to Chicago from that initial workup. Turner had suggested—had in fact urged it strongly and arranged it by telephone—that I stop at the hospital to visit Marcy Rankins, the gender-program coordinator. The treatment of transsexuals usually rests in the hands of men, who may feel compassion for their patients but can never share their craving for womanhood. So a woman is almost always kept on hand to soothe emotional patients, take care of the correspondence, and serve as a sounding board for the men's judgment of femininity. Pomeroy had brought in a woman colleague to second his recommendation of me for surgery. The Harry Benjamin establishment couldn't have existed without Virginia Allen, who had been adviser and mother confessor to a thousand transsexuals, myself included.

Marcy was special. She is young, pretty, and high-spirited, and with this she combines an intuition that is at times absolutely eerie. No matter how I might try to bluff her, she always knew what I was thinking and feeling. She has left Edgerton now and moved to Texas, but we keep in touch.

Marcy had arranged my schedule for the initial workup but had fallen ill just before I arrived, and Turner, whose patient she was, had thrown her into the hospital. There I met her for the first time, she in a pretty blue robe and I in a heavy wool coat. I adored her on sight. Within thirty seconds we were close friends, gabbing and laughing and exchanging secrets.

I assume that Edgerton and his associates sought Marcy's

views when they met two weeks later to decide my case, though I don't know this for a fact. Despite the pain and setbacks I was to endure, I have been grateful for their acceptance. But I have been proud of Marcy's approval. She is a total woman, and after all, it takes one to know one.

TWELVE

On Christmas Eve, Marcy sat down at her typewriter and wrote me: "We have arranged some operating time for you. There will be two stages, the first of which we would like to perform on February 17th, and the second stage on March 9th. I have arranged for your admission on the 16th of February. . . ."

I had won. I had broken through the last barrier, and in six weeks time I would be relieved of that despised encumbrance.

I was in the midst of the Christmas holidays, the happiest I had ever known. Ellen had disinterred the plastic Christmas tree from the basement and together we had decorated it with the tiny Italian lights, the silver garland, and the ornaments she had packed away with such care the year before and the years before that. Crèche figures made out of straw stood atop the piano; a Christmas candle adorned the record cabinet; a wreath hung on the front door. In all three rooms of the apartment her hands had brought or fashioned some touch of Christmas. The presents she had were concealed from me behind the right-hand bedroom curtain, mine were hidden from her behind the portable typewriter under my desk. I did not allow myself to think about the seasons to come when I would be alone, but Ellen touched on the matter one evening as we were having cocktails by the glitter of our Christmas tree.

"I'll be moving into an apartment of my own pretty soon," she said.

A feeling of such dread seized my stomach that I was almost sick.

"Do you have to talk about that just now?" I protested.

"Don't worry about it," she said. "I'm not going to leave you for six months or a year anyway."

As it happened, she moved out two months after I returned from the hospital.

I disinterred the plastic Christmas tree myself the next year and decorated it alone. I knew that Ellen would not come to see it; she was spending Christmas with her parents in New England. My Christmas presents for her were hidden again behind the portable typewriter under my desk, though I had no one from whom to hide them now. There were no presents from her to me. I didn't put out the crèche figures on top of the piano, and I couldn't find the Christmas candle. (That still happened to me quite often—I couldn't find things that Ellen had stored away.)

We had always started opening presents days before we should, not because we were greedy for what we were going to get but because we loved to see how the other would receive what was given. That was all right; we gave each other enough presents to last for several evenings. That last Christmas together, Ellen gave me eight presents, among them a silver ring with a green stone, a silk scarf, a pair of jade earrings, and a red shirt-jacket she had been making secretly.

There were Christmas parties we attended together and a midnight church service by candlelight with most of my favorite carols and a sermon that offended Ellen's Unitarian theology. I roasted a turkey with sausage stuffing, and we drank to each other's happiness with champagne.

Except for her reference to getting an apartment of her own, she gave no hint of what I now believe must have been a very deep unhappiness. I was so immersed in my own joy at my approaching surgical liberation that I didn't guess her misery or her eagerness to leave me.

And I had much cause to be happy in those days. The guys in the newsroom were treating me like a queen. Edgerton and Marcy awaited me at the University of Virginia to lead me into the world of biological womanhood. And at home there was yet Ellen—for "six months or a year." I didn't permit myself to think beyond that.

I flew down to Virginia on February 15. The Charlottesville airport has a sign that reads, WELCOME TO CHARLOTTESVILLE, HOME OF THE VIRGINIA CAVALIERS. Because I hadn't yet made many friends at the medical center, I dined alone that evening and went to bed early in the Howard Johnson's motel. We had planned that Ellen would fly down with me, but because she had fallen ill with flu, she had taken an extra day in bed; I expected her down the next afternoon. I was excited, even exhilarated, but not very scared —not as scared as I would have been if I had known what lay ahead.

The next morning I had my interview with the psychiatrist, the one I had missed when I had come down for my workup two months before. It was an empty gesture and an unpleasant experience. "It's too late now," he told me. "You're being admitted to the hospital this afternoon, and tomorrow morning they're going to cut your penis off!"

Thank heavens! I sighed to myself.

Most of the afternoon was consumed by the admissions process: filling out forms, X-rays, blood tests, urinalysis, blood pressure. A clerk fastened a plastic I.D. bracelet around my wrist. "University of Virginia Hospital—Nancy Hunt—Plastic Surgery," it read. I would wear it for the next twenty-nine days.

It was growing dark outside when they led me to my room and left me alone. Ellen's plane should have arrived two hours before, but there was no sign of her yet. The walls of the room were green, decorated with a very bad painting, a television set on a chrome-plated rack opposite the foot of the bed, and a basin and mirror in one corner. One door led to a toilet to be shared with the occupant of the next room. The window looked out on a grassy bank, now yellow in the dormancy of winter, surmounted by a row of brick buildings. I stared out the window, looking for Ellen.

I was finishing my supper of fried fish and carrots when at last I saw her on the sidewalk directly beneath my window. Even in February's early darkness, I could see that her face was drawn and ill, her walk heavy and dispirited. She had always had a curiously youthful gait—it reminded me of a high school adolescent's—and I used to take a secret pleasure in watching her lope along the sidewalk. She was plodding now. After threading her way through the corridors she found me, but there was no joy in her greeting. She had arrived; she had done what was required of her.

I put on the gray hospital gown that was to be my costume for the next four weeks, and Ellen tied it in the back. We settled down for an evening of distracted conversation, but were interrupted by several visitors, and presently Ellen departed, weary and ashen, for the motel. Edgerton stopped in to sit by my bed and infuse me with his confidence. A medical student came to take my history and perform a physical exam. The aide came to remove my supper tray. The anesthesiologist came to explain how I would be put to sleep the next day. A nurse came to administer a laxative and returned later to give me enemas. A student nurse came, somewhat apprehensively, to say that her name was Beth Forbes and she had chosen me as her study project and would be accompanying me to the operating room in the morning. Futrell came to ask me how I was feeling. Marsh came to tell me that he would be with me in the operating room and assure me that I would be all right. The nurse returned to say that any money in excess of five dollars would have to go in the hospital safe along with any valuable jewelry.

It was after eleven o'clock before they left me alone to climb into bed and turn out my light. I lay in the dark, listening to the rush of the air conditioning through a grille above the door. The room was already cold, and I had only a single light blanket. I had declined any medication to make me sleep, but though I was exhausted from my flight and the laxatives and enemas, I was too cold to sleep.

I should be thinking profoundly about my life and the strange turn that it will take tomorrow, I told myself. I remembered that on the night before her operation, Jan Morris had arisen from her bed in Casablanca and stood before a mirror to bid farewell to her male genitalia. A quixotic gesture, I thought. I didn't give a damn if I never saw mine again, and I certainly had no intention of arising in that frigid room to bid them good-bye.

A quick tap on the door was followed by the glare of the ceiling light. "Did you have blood work and a chest X-ray this afternoon?" It was the medical student who had examined me a few hours before. I told him I had. "Okay, I guess they'll send up the results pretty soon. Good-night."

I pulled the flimsy blanket more tightly about my neck. Gosh it was cold! It was just plain crazy to run that air conditioner full blast in the dead of winter. Americans have a thing about air conditioning, I thought balefully. If I'm going to spend God knows how many days in this room, I may survive the operation, but I'll certainly die of pneumonia. But at least it takes my mind off the surgery. Now if only I could get a little sleep before they come for me with the tumbril. . . .

Another quick tap on the door was again followed by the glare of the ceiling light. "We forgot to have you sign these forms. This one gives us permission to administer anesthesia, and this one authorizes the surgery. . . ."

Darkness again. Cold again. Shivering now in the relentless blast of the air conditioning, I decided I should have taken a sleeping pill. But who could sleep with this Rotary Club convention going on in here? Here on the bleak, windswept Russian steppes with the snow crystals cutting the flesh raw and the pitiless howl of the wolves in the distance. . . .

I found the call box pinned to the head of my bed and pressed the button.

"Can I help you?" A quiet, English-accented voice, here in the heart of the tundra?

"May I have another blanket?" I asked piteously.

Soon another knock on the door, but this time the ceiling light didn't come on. "Hello," said the pleasant English voice, "I'm Eileen Brindley, the ward secretary. I'm just going off duty now, so I thought I'd bring you the blanket myself and see how you're getting on." She spread a double thickness of blanket over me as she talked, and I began to feel warmth seep back into my bones. "This is an old building, and we have a lot of trouble with the air conditioning. There, is that better now? Can I get you anything else? I won't keep you awake any longer, but I did want to meet you. Good-night, sleep well."

I stretched luxuriously, feeling my body relax. What a nice woman! No matter what the others might or might not think about me and my quest, at least she bore me no malice. Perhaps the others didn't either. They see a lot of queer things in hospitals, transsexuals included. Maybe it doesn't bother them. I'm just one more surgical patient, as far as they're concerned. One more routine case. Nothing to worry about.

And at last I was asleep.

Ellen returned in the morning. The dark rings under her eyes contrasted shockingly with the pallor of her face, but I had no strength to give her. I had had no breakfast, an omission that always makes me cross and absentminded. And I was already beginning to lose my grasp on events. They would be coming for me soon; the best I could do to help them was to submit passively, to shut up and do what I was told. In that condition, I could hardly assert my love and support. For that matter, I could have used some love and support myself, but she had little enough to spare.

The student nurse entered in her blue-and-white uniform and starched cap: Beth—dark-haired, straight-backed, pretty, with an expression that combined determination and youthful vulnerability. What does she see here in this room? A sexual freak about to undergo an unspeakable operation? Two women in strained conversation? A man and his wife parting? I gazed into her dark eyes and could not read their meaning. But I could feel her strength, steady and gentle. Here was a hand I could cling to as they took me away.

Presently the head nurse entered, armed with two syringes, one for each hip, the first to relax me and the second to dry up my secretions. Two orderlies arrived, their heads and necks swathed in green, like men from Mars. They braced their cart against the side of my bed. No rings on? No earrings? No contact lenses? No nail polish? All right, scoot yourself over this way. That's good, not too fast. We don't want you to land on the floor. Now your feet.

They covered me with a sheet, raised the rails on either side, and rolled me out of the room. Ellen remained behind. She could not help me, I could not help her. Let her go. The medication was already disorienting me. I seemed to glide through the corridors in the center of a little crowd: the orderlies in their frightening green headgear, the nurses, the passersby who parted on either side to let us through. Beth was walking by my head, her face solemn but serene. I tried to keep track of the corners that we turned, the doors that we passed, the elevators that we entered and left, but I couldn't keep them all straight. I was lost, spinning and careening beneath a procession of lights. Look at Beth. Keep looking. Her position does not alter. She is always there by your head, and she is not afraid. Ellen.

The cart slid into a tiny, yellow-tiled alcove. For a few minutes, there in semidarkness, I was alone. Then there was a cool, wet swab on the back of my left hand. "Now you're going to feel a little bee-sting." It was the last thing I felt for seven hours.

I had thought of a joke to say when I woke up. I had even rehearsed it to myself to make sure I had it right. Parodying the stereotypical cancer patient, I intended to flutter my eyelids weakly and ask in a quivering voice, "Doctor, are you sure you got it all?"

But as it happened, I awoke in such a stupor that my mind could handle only the most primitive thoughts: need to pee; it's gotten dark outside already, must be late; the room is rolling around; operation must be over; lots of people in here; where's Ellen?; need to pee.

When they had arranged me to their satisfaction, when they had installed all the plastic plumbing and put up the side rails, when Ellen had replaced my pierced earrings (as I had insisted she do, fearing that the newly augered holes in my earlobes would close up), when everyone had departed, I tried to concentrate on the significance of what had been done to me. I knew that I should regard this an awesome act, decisive in my life, but I just couldn't manage it.

Though I worked at it off and on for several days, I simply couldn't make myself feel that I had undergone anything more earthshaking than the removal of a troublesome appendix or the correction of a set of webbed toes. Taken as an emotional experience, the surgery came as an anticlimax. Ellen was probably more profoundly affected than I. She called on me morning and afternoon, arranging the contents of my suitcase and fussing about my room, her face ravaged more by psychological trauma than by the remnants of her flu. A day earlier than we had planned, she flew back to Chicago to lick her wounds. My own wounds were surgical and were thought to be healing normally.

Aesthetically, however, I had suffered a reversal. The hospital gown did not flatter my figure; my hair was a mess; my face looked like a fallen soufflé; and I had no energy to apply makeup or even put on my contact lenses. My voice, which I had cultivated in a more feminine register, emerged now as a rasping croak, the result of prolonged intubation on the operating table. For several days, I tried not to call the nurses because I didn't want them to hear that gravelly discord.

And when the dressings were changed, I could scarcely force myself to survey the bloody field of battle. Everything was at sixes and sevens. Here was no classic mold of womanly beauty but rather a tattered mixture of the old and the new, the male and the female, the ugly and the beautiful. I was suspended halfway between two surgical procedures, neither man nor woman. I had not prepared myself for that spectacle, and I found it shocking.

Worse, I feared it would shock my friends, of whom I was gathering a close circle. They were mostly third-year clinical nursing students—college juniors by ordinary reckoning, all of them young enough to be my daughters with a few years to spare: first Beth, then Marcia and Jennifer and Lynn. With whatever apprehension, each in turn would choose me as her special project for the morning—to bathe me and make my bed and change my dressings, to take my vital signs and fiddle with my I.V.—always under the eye of an instructor who could scarcely have been five years older than they. They were all lovely young women, serious but not yet hardened to the grotesques of hospital life, and I tried to be a model patient for them.

I worried about how I might affect their attitudes toward men. They were themselves still growing into womanhood and susceptible to trauma. How might they feel about men to see me, a deserter from the male ranks, with the torn and gory remnants of my male anatomy still clinging to my body? What shock and revulsion might fill them as they removed my dressings and irrigated my ghastly wound?

If they were appalled, they took care not to show it. I would watch their faces as they removed the four-by-four gauze sponges and with infinite gentleness irrigated the surgical site. Their eyes remained steady—concerned, but undismayed.

I wanted above all else to be admitted to the society of women, and of these nursing students in particular. Yet my own womanly credentials were belied by the revelation of my masculine stigmata, still incompletely excised. Would it make a joke of my claim to sisterhood? On the contrary, they welcomed me at once. They would return to visit me when they had completed their morning rounds or during the afternoon or even afer supper, and we would talk and giggle and reveal our dreams and fears. Sometimes I would ask about my new anatomy in the making, or what it was like to love a man. Our conversation ranged across the whole spectrum of our experience: hospitals, newspapers, ballet, automobiles, skiing, parents—anything we cared about. Sometimes, in the evening, these talks lasted for hours.

Often they showed me kindness far beyond the requirements of nursing or even of friendship. They would shop for me or wash my hair. Once when I complained about the impossibility of shaving my legs in bed, their instructor came back to my room on her own time and did that for me too. I floated on the great ocean of their charity. When, in the middle of my hospitalization, they all went home for spring vacation, my social life collapsed and I endured a week of un-utterable gloom. The night that vacation ended, Jennifer bounded into my room to tell me about her week in Chicago, and I was so glad to see her I almost cried.

Others befriended me as well. Two speech therapists called almost daily to drill me in feminine elocution with a tape recorder, pitch pipe, and word lists. Brindley, the ward secretary, stopped by to chat, often bringing me presents, and sometimes she would sit beside my bed and knit while we talked about England and her children. Brindley it was who insisted on having the doctors order beer for me. "Of course you should have beer since you like it. No, it's no trouble at all. They have it and can quite easily send it up, and we can keep it in the refrigerator by the nurses' station. So that's settled, then." It was, too. Brindley had two cans of beer a day sent up for me, and if they failed to arrive, she got on the phone and raised hell until they appeared. I drank one can every night at nine o'clock and saved the other for entertaining friends. If you cannot have a mother with you, you can do no better than to rely on dear Brindley.

There was a man, too, the first man I ever cared for deeply. He would stop by almost every afternoon or evening, sometimes still in his operating-room greens with the cap on his gray hair and the surgical mask hanging beneath his beautiful face. We would split a can of beer in paper cups and discuss English literature, about which he knew vastly more than I. One crisp and glorious afternoon, when I had sufficiently recovered to dress and leave the hospital for a few hours, he drove me out to Jefferson's Monticello. He never kissed me on the lips, but he did once hold me in his arms, and briefly I sensed what it must feel like to be cherished and safe.

I have been back to Charlottesville several times and have always been happy to see my friends, and I have corresponded with two or three of them. But their lives have gone on their separate ways, and so has mine. They touched me once and illuminated my life. When I remember those four weeks in the hospital, I do not think about the frightening procession to the operating room, the horror of being laced in my bed by a maze of plastic tubing, the pain as I forced myself to trudge from end to end of the corridor, over and over, with the bag of urine from my catheter dangling at my wrist like an obscene purse. I think of the people who accepted me as a woman at a time when acceptance was my greatest need.

A week or so after that first operation, I returned to the operating room to have the internal packing removed. Again the pre-op shots in the buttocks, again the supine ride through the corridors, again the "little bee-sting" in the back of the left hand, followed by oblivion. In most sex-reassignment procedures, the packing is removed without anesthetic, and the experience can be excruciatingly painful.

Yet again at the end of the third week I was taken to the operating room and shoved over the brink of insensibility while the surgeons performed Step II and tidied up the mess they had previously made. When I awoke—throat sore, mouth parched—I asked for a can of beer both to quench my thirst and to celebrate what I believed was the completion of the project. That was a mistake on two counts: the beer made me sick to my stomach, and the surgery would turn out badly.

On the twenty-ninth day, they discharged me. Futrell gave me a final examination and seemed surprised that I complained of so much pain. I said good-bye to Marcy—we hugged each other and she said that if I cried she was going to break my neck—and had a farewell lunch with one of the student nurses. Then the taxi came and drove me away, and as I glanced out the rear window at the receding red-brick building of the medical center, the tears welled up in my eyes until they threatened to dislodge my contacts.

The American Airlines flight from Washington to Chicago was full that night, and the stewardesses found themselves short just one supper. I don't know how they made their choice, but out of possibly two hundred passengers I was designated as the one who wouldn't eat. Perhaps it stemmed from the fact that, having lost eight pounds and looking like a badly preserved cadaver, I was plainly the one most accustomed to going hungry. I was in a good deal of pain and not at all sure that I could last the flight in a sitting position, so while the other passengers ate, I dulled my misery with bourbon, the first liquor I had tasted in a month. Then American Airlines mislaid my suitcase and I had to wait in the terminal at Chicago for an hour and a half until they found it, meanwhile drinking more bourbon provided by an attentive ex–Air Force flier. At least my talent for getting picked up by fliers had not deserted me.

By the time I reached home, therefore, I was feeling very ill indeed, and moreover I was breaking out in hives. Ellen fed me and put me to bed, but her efficiency was untempered by gentleness. She was doing her duty, nothing more. I remembered the same coldness when I had returned from the Middle East: the same gulf between us, the same awareness that something was terribly wrong. I remembered too the same emotional shriveling that had occurred when she had gone away to Norway years before. Now, on top of the fact that I had ceased to be her husband and had followed my own destiny at the price of our marriage, she showed me the barren truth: whenever we were apart too long, her af-

209

fection could not bridge the gulf. She later blamed me for this during a quarrel. "You went away and left me for four weeks," she said reproachfully. My month's absence in the hospital represented the ultimate betrayal.

As a nurse, however, she took a clinical interest in the surgical results. She looked up a textbook illustration with which she compared the job and admired the realism that had been achieved. She swabbed the incision lines with peroxide to remove the clots, and as the catgut sutures softened and broke down in the proper manner, she plucked them out as if she were tweezing an eyebrow. She comforted me with reassuring words.

But doubts assailed me. The pain didn't abate. When I returned to the newsroom, I could barely force myself to endure the agony of sitting, and often I finished the night's work kneeling on my chair. Supper hours I spent lying on the couch in the ladies' room lounge.

"If there's one thing that really makes me mad," said a tough little reporter who found me there one evening, "it's women who goof off in here, lying on that sofa."

"Gosh, Carol," I said in my most femininely ineffectual voice, "in my present status I hardly know what to tell you. A year ago I would have told you to go fuck yourself."

Although I had expected some postoperative discomfort, nothing had prepared me for the unremitting pain. I couldn't survive the night without Valium.

"You've got to expect it after surgery," Ellen said. "It's nothing to worry about. You're healing fine."

But I wasn't healing fine. I was beginning to drain.

"I think maybe I ought to see a doctor," I said.

"You can if you want to, but there's absolutely nothing the matter with you. It just takes time."

I hadn't been home a month before she began looking for an apartment of her own. "What happened to 'six months or a year'?" I asked.

"New leases begin May first," she said. "That is the best time to find an apartment."

Perversely I accompanied her on her apartment hunting, walking ten or fifteen blocks at a time and trying to forget how much I hurt. I also began trying to find a gynecologist who would see me right away, not having learned that gynecologists schedule their new patients six weeks to two months in advance. I finally tracked down a man who had been a member of the gender team at Northwestern Memorial Hospital and was offered an appointment for six weeks hence. When I pleaded that I was in deep trouble and really wanted to see him urgently, his secretary implied that I'd better watch my manners or she wouldn't let me see him at all. I took the appointment, but then went to the emergency room of the hospital down the block from our apartment and got myself on a week's course of antibiotics. When that didn't stop the pain and infection, I went back for another week of the same thing.

Ellen finally settled for an apartment across the street in the same building where we had first lived together. She would be able to look out her windows at night and see my lights, and I could see hers. She told me that, apart from her own belongings, she intended to take almost none of our furniture with her. I had paid for it, and she didn't want it. She planned to decorate her place on an entirely different theme—something Chinese-y, she thought, with sleeping mats on the floor and possibly a fountain and a rock garden in one corner.

When the time came, what little she took she carried over

herself: her clothes; the stereo, which her father had given to her as a graduation present; the sewing machine that had once belonged to her mother and on which she had taught me to sew; the little desk and chair I had given her during our first winter together; the down sleeping bag I had bought her for our camping trip to the Rockies and that now would be her bed on the floor; the brass candlesticks that had been a Christmas present to us both.

But she left much of herself behind: the big, unabridged Random House dictionary she had had in college; the flute she had played in high school; the captain's chair with her university's shield on the back that I had given her to match my chair from Yale; the houseplants she had bought and always cared for; the needlepoint bellpull in the front hall; the copy of *Gone With the Wind* that she had cherished since she was a child. Everywhere I looked, my eye fell—as it still does—on something that Ellen once owned and left behind.

She moved out for good one evening while I was at work. I grieved as I climbed the stairs that night, knowing that she would not be there. I turned on the lights, then locked and chained the door. The apartment had never seemed so empty. I walked from room to room, looking for signs of her departure. Really, she had taken so little that her absence could scarcely be noticed. The place was mine now, almost exactly as we had arranged it together over the years.

I walked into the bedroom at last, flicked on the light, and there I found the definitive sign of her departure. My jewelry box stood open on the bureau, and tossed into its bottom tier lay Ellen's diamond engagement ring. Plainly she would have no further use for it.

The first few weeks of solitude nearly drove me mad. To lose one's dearest friend and best companion is more than a traumatic amputation; it's a form of blinding, a deprivation of the senses, as if a bat were to lose the echo-ranging ability by which it navigates in dark caverns, or a dolphin the beeps that help guide it through the watery world. If I spoke, I received no echo; if I listened, I heard no beep. My beacons had fallen silent, and I dared not fly for fear of crashing.

I hated to return to the silence of the apartment. I hated to sleep alone. The mornings I could bear, the afternoons and evenings offered the anodyne of work; but the nights were awful. I lay awake for hours, throbbing with postoperative pain and twisting on the spit of loneliness. Most insupportable were the days off from work, and to fill these voids I contrived an elaborate social schedule of entertaining or dining out with friends. More than six weeks passed before I hazarded an entire twenty-four hours alone.

Doubts of my self-sufficiency crowded me. Ellen had always taken the laundry to the laundromat, having evolved a procedure founded on various combinations of detergent, bleaches, fabric softener, and different water temperatures that she didn't think I could master. I didn't think so either. Ellen had always supervised the cleaning of the apartment; now the responsibility was mine. In that first week, I scoured the kitchen walls and cabinets until they gleamed, not out of a mania for cleanliness but merely to prove to myself that I could at least do one household job better than Ellen. It was four months, however, before I mustered the nerve to wash and iron the dining room and bedroom curtains, having feared all that time that I might not be able to hang them again precisely as Ellen had. I was determined to maintain the apartment just as Ellen had left it, and so I became not a housekeeper but the curator of a shrine.

What was true for the apartment held truer still for myself. As a woman, I was largely the creation of Ellen's hands. It was she who had pressed my dresses, had tied the bow at my neck and the ribbon in my hair, had guided me in the selection of my clothes. Until she left, I had never used a blow-dryer; she had always done my hair. I wasn't sure I could continue to dress myself, so utterly dependent on her had I become as a woman.

We had agreed on parting that we would remain friends, and at first we tried. Ellen kept her keys to my apartment and said she would give me a key to hers. We planned to spend our summer vacations together. We would dine together often. But the arrangement soured from the start. Though she came to supper whenever I invited her, she never invited me in return. Though she kept her keys to my apartment, she never offered me one to hers. Though I had scheduled my summer vacation to coincide with hers, she said she wouldn't go. The terms of our accommodation were shifting faster than I could keep up with, and I was thrown off balance. She had always been a rock of trustworthiness; now she broke her word as casually as she drew breath. Neither explanation nor apology was made, so total was her rejection of the values we once had shared. "I don't have to live by your standards," she said. "You're not my judge."

The fights were the worst of all. In seven years together we had seldom quarreled, and when we had the fault had been mine more often than hers. She had brought to our marriage not only an innate capacity for love but also a resourceful intelligence. When love failed to heal our differences, she used her brains. She always knew what I was thinking, often before I knew it myself, and could submerge her own rancor to bring us peace. Sometimes I became so intrigued by the ingenuity she applied to this task that I deliberately prolonged an argument for the delight of watching her solve the problem. She could play me no less deftly than she played the soprano recorder, like a virtuoso.

So I was ill-equipped to deal with the fights that now erupted. I didn't understand their cause nor know how to end them. Suddenly, inexplicably, an amicable conversation would turn into a blazing row, and I couldn't perceive how the trick was done.

One night I had invited her to supper. We were having after-dinner coffee by candlelight, she in her captain's chair and I in mine, just as we had sat together in harmony a thousand times before. And as had happened so often, I was telling her why I admired and loved her. Unexpectedly, she blazed up at me.

"I don't have to sit here and take that from you!" she cried, shoving her chair violently backward as she stood up.

"What are you talking about?" I asked incredulously. "I was only telling you how much I admire you."

But now her tongue was unbridled. She began carrying dishes out to the sink and washing them as if she still lived there, meanwhile berating me for a dozen sins, some real and others imagined. As her fury rose, I retreated into the darkened living room. She continued her list of accusations, her voice raised so that I might not miss any detail of her indictment. I had cheated her, she said. I had kept her personal property in my apartment. I had withheld money that was rightfully hers.

The fact was that with her keys she could enter the apartment whenever she chose and take anything she wanted, and with her signature she could take every penny I had, since I had left our joint checking and savings accounts intact. Moreover she knew that I would begrudge her nothing.

We had made a friendly divorce agreement, if not a wise one. A few weeks before my surgery, we had gone to the lawyer who had liberated me from my first marriage. He had often told me that he didn't believe in one lawyer representing both sides in a divorce, but since we appeared to be on such good terms and Ellen was asking so little, he agreed to do the job for us. I had given the matter slight thought. To me the divorce was nothing but a prerequisite to the surgery. No court action, I thought, could affect the real ties that bound us together. But to Ellen the divorce was real enough, though I didn't know it at the time. Later I was surprised to find in her apartment books on the agony of severing a marriage.

"I'm going to hire a clever lawyer and make you pay!" she was shouting from the kitchen.

"And I'm going to hire a clever lawyer and stop you!" I choked.

Then she was standing beside me in the dark, her hand caressing my shoulder. "There, there, don't cry," she said. "It's all right, it's all right. I'm sorry. Don't cry."

After she had left, I sat a long time in the dark, forcing myself to face the truth that I had long denied: We were finished. We must let each other go. We were strangling each other, I with dependence, she with reproach. If I was now the woman that I had aspired to be, I must learn to make that woman brave. Ellen was fighting for independence, and I must accept the same for myself. I must find the courage to cut us loose.

One thing was certain: I was fed up with apologizing. I could not, would not, crawl through the rest of my life begging forgiveness for an affliction that had been visited on me and that I would have preferred to forgo. Society in general and my family in particular had assumed that transsexualism was a form of self-indulgence, a pleasure for me at their expense.

What about your wife? people invariably asked on learning of my disorder.

Their question had two levels of meaning. On the first, they wanted to know if we were continuing our sex life. On the second, they wanted to know how I could possibly justify the terrible thing that I was doing to her. It was a question they wouldn't have dared ask if I'd said I had cancer of the prostate.

Underlying their inquisitiveness was the assumption that it's an amusing caprice for a middle-aged man to turn into a woman. It certainly has been a frequent theme of comedy since the Norse sagas and continuing down to *Charley's Aunt* and Milton Berle. But what is funny on the stage is no joy in reality. People who assumed that I had embarked on this course on a whim were simply mistaken.

Ellen knew this, of course. More than that, she had helped release me from the rack of manhood. She had aided and abetted my escape, finding a measure of enjoyment in the early stages but knowing that she would regret it. She had done it anyway, out of love for me and repugnance toward the suffering of a fellow human being. And she was suffering now, to my grief and remorse. But I was not going to do everlasting penance. For my own sanity as well as hers, there had to be an end to flagellation.

She came over a few afternoons later to pick up some more things: the sewing box, the steam iron, the Bishop Method sewing book. It took her several trips to carry everything across the street.

"I want your keys to this apartment," I told her.

217

There were more of them than I had remembered: keys to the front door downstairs, the apartment, the back door, the basement door, the areaway door. She flung them down on my desk and started out. "Good luck!" she said angrily.

"Wait a second. There are still a lot of your things here."

"Anything I haven't taken now," she answered, "you can burn."

"I'm sorry we're ending like this," I said lamely. "I guess Noël Coward farewells only happen in the theater."

"I'm sorry too," she snapped, and was gone forever.

THIRTEEN

Shortly after Ellen's departure, I finally had my audience with the gynecologist. Not only did he dislike transsexuals, but he was also openly disdainful of the surgery that had been performed on me.

"Where did you have this done?" he asked contemptuously, as if I were some unpleasant object he was turning over with his foot.

I told him, but he appeared not to know that the University of Virginia was performing sex-reassignment surgery.

"What's the name of your surgeon down there?"

The name I gave meant nothing to him, which I thought odd because Edgerton had pioneered sex-reassignment surgery in this country and had appeared frequently in the literature.

"You realize, of course," he continued, "that this vagina is incapable of intercourse."

I hadn't realized it—hadn't even considered the possibility. I had assumed that once the infection was controlled, I would be able to function fully as a woman.

"What you've got here is nothing but a sinus—a sort of little tube like this." He held up a finger to demonstrate the size. "Besides, it enters at the wrong angle—like this instead of like this. Now as a married man, you can understand the impossibility of having intercourse with a vagina like that."

It was the third time he had prefaced a remark with the phrase *as a married man,* and I was ready to strangle him. He hadn't even known I was a transsexual when he first saw me in bra and panties.

I left his office in a state of misery approaching shock. It had all been in vain, I thought numbly: the twenty-nine days in the hospital and the two operations and the months of pain. I remained an incomplete woman. I didn't know what to do. A month before I would have told Ellen, and she would have comforted me and suggested some course of action. But Ellen was lost to me now, and I would have to solve my own problems. About time, too.

I brooded for a week and then wrote Marcy one of my immensely long letters.

"I'm determined to keep going," I concluded, "which is getting harder to do all the time. . . . The pain keeps me awake at night, and as the sleep deficit mounts, I grow crabbier and less efficient at my job. The problems of personal cleanliness are almost insurmountable . . . . all of this inspires a sense of such futility and despair that I narcotize myself with two packs of cigarettes a day and far more alcohol than is good for me. Newspaper people tend to drink a lot anyway, and the guys I date—all newspapermen—don't offer much entertainment except bar-hopping." The suggestion that I was dating lots of newspapermen was pure bravado. Sunk into gloom and self-absorption, I had become unfit company for anyone, and men and women alike had consigned me to social isolation.

I waited a decent interval for Marcy to digest my morose letter, then called her long-distance.

"Poor Nancy," she commiserated, "you're really having a rough time, aren't you. Would you like to come down here to the clinic on Tuesday?"

Yes, I would like that.

The next Tuesday, Edgerton and Futrell examined me, murmuring medically to each other behind the sheet that draped my legs. As they peered more deeply, I writhed in pain and clutched the nurse's hand. "Breathe real deep, honey," she said. "That helps." And it did.

"There appears to have been some stenosis during the healing process," Edgerton told me, referring to a narrowing of the vaginal introitus, or orifice. "But I think we can relieve that and give you what you want. I'd like you to come back here in September and let us operate on you again. We'll keep you in the hospital about a week or ten days. Bill, I'll want you in on this, and you might get in touch with Jim Turner and ask him to be in the operating room to help us out." Turner was the team gynecologist.

I asked Edgerton if he thought that in my present condition I could make love with a man. He said he didn't think so.

It's a curious human characteristic that what seems insupportable one day becomes bearable and even desirable the next. I hadn't thought I could endure another operation: the preoperative shots, the dismal progression through the corridors, the little bee-sting on the back of the left hand, the dizzying climb back to consciousness, the days of recovery and dressing changes, the catheter, the boredom. Now I looked forward to it as I would the Second Coming.

"Do you think you can make it till September?" Edgerton asked.

Two more months of pain and drainage. Two more months of delay in fulfillment as a woman. "I guess so," I said ruefully. I didn't have much choice.

A week before the scheduled surgery, Edgerton's office called. "I'm afraid we've got some bad news. We're going to have to postpone your operation until the end of October." They told me there were difficulties with Futrell's schedule.

"You can't," I wailed.

But they could. Though I pleaded and threatened and wept, they remained adamant. (The same thing happened to another transsexual I know, and produced the same reaction. Having pinned hopes and work schedule and college curriculum on a surgery date, she telephoned me at the office in such a state of despair that I was concerned for what she might do. Transsexuals base their expectations on their operations, and they react badly when the promise of surgical relief is unexpectedly postponed.)

I could think of no recourse. Edgerton would probably not have countenanced the postponement, but he was in Scotland and beyond my reach.

In a final attempt to avoid postponement, I telephoned Futrell at his home and pleaded with him to operate on the originally scheduled day. "There's this guy I've been seeing, and I really like him," I explained.

"Have you been drinking?" Futrell demanded, probably annoyed that I had called him at home to appeal his decision.

"No!" I wailed. I was, in fact, just on my way to work.

"I don't know why you're so eager to have this operation," Futrell said. "It's not going to accomplish a great deal."

"Well, at least I'll be able to put out," I answered.

"I doubt it very much."

"But Bill," I protested, "you and Dr. Edgerton said it would turn out all right."

"I doubt it very much," he repeated maddeningly.

The room was tilting crazily about me. "You can't do this," I said. "I've got everything scheduled to take sick leave from work and the landlady coming in to water my plants . . . you said you'd operate on me."

"I wouldn't operate on you now no matter what," he retorted.

"But Bill, you and Dr. Edgerton promised. Somebody down there has got to keep their word!"

As it turned out, they did. Two days later, Edgerton's office called to say that the original date for the surgery had been reinstated.

So on September 13, I was back in the hospital and glad to be there. The night before the operation, Jennifer bounded into my room. A student of the dance, she did not merely walk into a room but invariably entered with a grand jeté. We hadn't seen each other since my discharge that March, and though we had corresponded voluminously all summer, we rejoiced to see each other. We hugged and laughed in sheer delight and each tried to outtalk the other, to the dismay of the intern who was trying to take a patient-history from me.

The next afternoon as I emerged from the fog of halothane, I saw the beautiful face of my gray-haired scholar of English literature. He must have been waiting for me, and I

223

longed to reach out for his embrace, though I had enough sense to know even in my befuddled state that I mustn't do so, not in front of this throng of surgeons and nurses installing me amid the now familiar network of plastic tubing.

The day after that, Marcia and Lynn came by to visit, and there was a vase of red roses from Jennifer.

Like most hospitals, the University of Virginia takes its surgical patients from the operating room to the recovery room and keeps them there until they awake enough to demonstrate that their brains are functioning. This is usually established by a series of simple questions: "What's your name?" "Do you know where you are?" "Where do you live?" Once the patient can answer these, she is taken to her room.

I had passed through the recovery room and undergone this interrogation after each of my previous operations, but I had never remembered it. This time I recalled it clearly. I opened my eyes and saw Marsh standing near my feet, grinning triumphantly. "It went really well," he said happily. "When we got in there, we found a sort of pocket at the apex that had been sealed off by the infection. We opened it up and did a skin graft, and you've got almost the full length of the original vagina." I closed my eyes and drifted contentedly back to sleep.

Futrell told me much the same thing a day or two later. "We cut in there," he said, "and this stuff like pus came spurting out."

It must have been a nasty moment for them, one they could not easily have foreseen. Until they made their incision, they couldn't look deep enough inside to learn exactly what had happened to their work since they had last operated on me six months before.

In his postoperative notes, Marsh described the sequence of events. "The patient was placed on the table in the supine position . . ." he began.

Ah, but I remembered that. I hadn't remembered the three previous times I'd been put on the table, but I recalled this one.

"Can you scoot yourself down to this end of the table?" someone had asked. "Hey! Hey! Not so fast. You'll go right off the end."

"Boy, that would annoy Futrell, wouldn't it?" I giggled.

I was surrounded by figures in operating-room greens with surgical masks over their noses and mouths. They were preparing for the work at hand, and unexpectedly one of them began to laugh. "Things were never like this in New Haven!" he said.

"Were you at Yale?" I babbled. "So was I. I got out of there in the Class of 1950. What year were you there?"

At that point somebody sent the unanswerable Mickey Finn sliding down the tube and into my veins.

Marsh's notes went on: ". . . and after satisfactory induction of general endotracheal anesthesia, the patient was put into lithotomy. The pubic hair was shaved and the lower abdomen and pubis and thighs were prepped with betadine. Inspection was undertaken which revealed midline stenosis of the labia and absence of vaginal vault. The midline was sharply divided and as the stenotic vault was opened a pocket containing greenish somewhat grumous material was entered. This then led to . . . the superior portion of the previously constructed vault. . . ."

The notes continued in this tone for several hundred words. "A #18 Foley was placed into the bladder to identify the course of the urethra, and the soft tissues were dissected releasing scar tissue and allowing expansion of the introitus and relieving the waste stenosis of the vault. . . .

"A split thickness skin graft $^{16}/_{1000}$ of an inch was taken with the Reese dermatome from the right posterior buttock and thigh. The graft was then tailored to cover the absent lining in the vault and the grafts were sewn in place using three segments. . . ."

And finally: "The patient tolerated the procedure well, there were no complications and there was no transfusion. She was transferred to the recovery room in good condition."

Marsh had had reason to grin. It was a very neat piece of work.

Two or three days later, I asked him, "Jeff, did you do that operation?" No matter whose name appears on the chart, you can't always be sure which surgeon did the job.

"Yes, I did it," Marsh said.

"Thanks a lot."

He grabbed my toes where they stuck up beneath the blanket and shook them gently. "Don't mention it," he said.

They kept me in the hospital for two more weeks. The afternoon before my discharge, my English scholar came to say good-bye, and I clung to him as if he belonged to me instead of to his wife, an allegiance he had made clear. I have met other men and gone to bed with some of them and loved one, but he was the first to touch my new spring of love. I don't think he guessed that until we said good-bye. It probably embarrassed him.

The day of my departure, Jennifer lunched with me at a restaurant near the hospital and took me to see her new apartment. She then walked back to the hospital with me, and we parted in one of the hundred corridors by a bank of elevators. I carried my suitcase out into the street, climbed into a cab, and drove out to the airport. The sign was still there: WELCOME TO CHARLOTTESVILLE, HOME OF THE VIRGINIA CAVALIERS. Again I took the Piedmont prop-jet to Washington National and transferred to the flight to Chicago, this time with enough suppers on board for everyone. It was dark when I landed. The taxi let me out at my door, and I looked up at my apartment windows. They were dark, of course. No one else lived there now.

FOURTEEN

I have tried hard to avoid the transsexual's stereotypical behavior: the unreliability and ingratitude and untruthfulness, as well as the inflated breasts, theatrical makeup, and ribbons and ruffles. And on the whole I have succeeded. But research indicates another common failing: Transsexuals are promiscuous, and in this particular I have not achieved a notable level of virtue.

A friend in the newsroom says that he has gone to bed with more than eighty women (and unintentionally with one preoperative transsexual, not me) and claims that he can remember all their names. I find this hard to believe. Eighty bed-partners, maybe, but to remember all their names? I can't even remember all the guys I've been in bed with, though I doubt they total more than a dozen or so. But I've been working at it for less than a year.

I know such promiscuity is neither safe nor sanitary, but transsexuals do have an urge to prove the utility of their new vaginas.

The procession into my bed began in that dismal summer after my first and unsuccessful round of surgery when I was full of pain. Edgerton had told me that my anatomy wouldn't function until it had been remodeled, and he was right, though I couldn't resist the temptation to find out for myself. Men would try with might and main, jabbing away at me until I was ready to cry with vexation and fatigue. Most of them knew nothing about me or my past and found it difficult to accept the fact that they had at last met a woman who couldn't be made. Their efforts hurt like hell and often left me bruised and sore for days.

The first was a *Tribune* printer, the second a probation officer, and the third an editor for the *Sun-Times*. After that I lost track. Some of them gave it up as a bad job at the outset and allowed us both to get some sleep. One swarthy little tavern-owner, on the other hand, demonstrated an astonishing tenacity and strove for hours with undiminished vigor. Most of them I met in the bar across the street from Tribune Tower, or in some other bar. I was very lonely at the time and drinking too much. One or two of them I liked, but few ever called me again after their humiliation in failing to assault my virtue.

Nor did my luck improve much after my second bout of surgery. The healing process requires a month or two, and after its completion I found that I was still exceedingly small. More men tried and failed again. Sex as a woman remained an obstacle for me, a test, an ordeal; pleasure it was not. I was embarrassed by my own incapacity and apologetic to my partner each time I defaulted on an implied contract. I had read about transsexuals savoring the joy of orgasm; I would have been happy just to part with my virginity, even if it hurt.

The man who finally succeeded where so many had not was a structural iron worker—Pete later called him "your steel-driving man"—who picked me up on Christmas Eve in the bar around the corner from where I lived. I had just gotten off work and couldn't face my apartment with the plastic Christmas tree and no presents from Ellen. My steel-driving man bought me a drink and told me about his son in college, and eventually I allowed him to take me home to bed. It was the best Christmas present I could have asked for, but grateful though I was, it was a mechanical achievement, empty of love.

After that, I tried to be more selective, not always successfully. There was the sales manager from Minneapolis who was in town for a week and who on the first night toppled backward out of bed onto the floor in the excitement of his ardor. There was the IBM trainee who displayed the most delightful technique until he discovered how small I was, whereupon he arose and dressed and went away, declaring that he was afraid he would hurt me and, worse still, was afraid he would hurt himself. There was the airline pilot who murmured endearments in Icelandic (that is, I assumed they were endearments) and then treacherously practiced coitus interruptus on me because "I do not want to give you a baby." There was the eighteen-year-old Puerto Rican boy who did it because he needed a place to spend the night.

But after the novelty had worn off, I settled down to relationships with just one man at a time, and of these there have been only two: both of them three or four years older than I, and both of them married.

Jack was an architect who lived with his wife and children in the suburbs but who had fixed up his office in town so that he could spend an occasional night there. He had installed leaded windows, a Dutch-tile fireplace, and a trick double bed that folded up into a cabinet. His cooking arrangements were masculine and inadequate, but he kept plenty of ice cubes and a good stock of liquor. Once or twice a week, he would phone me at the paper and say that he was staying the night in town and would I like to stop by after work for a nightcap. The wording of the invitation never changed much, nor did the program for the night. He always had something for me to eat when I got there: a pot of thick pea soup or a pastrami on pumpernickel or—if he had forgotten to plan ahead, as was often the case—some soggy matzos and a jar of cheese-spread that had been left uncovered in the refrigerator. Once he had a steak. But no matter how much I pouted or cajoled, he never had orange juice for the next morning. He didn't drink orange juice.

Most Thursday nights at 11:00 o'clock I would go straight from work to Jack's place. He would have it arranged like the stage set for a seduction scene: adjustable lights dimmed, fire lit, classical tape going on the stereo. A gigantic slug of bourbon—already poured over ice in a green glass as thick as a telephone-pole insulator—waited for me on the coffee table (made out of a ship's hatch cover). He would bring out my hot soup (he seldom had any himself) and talk about my writing or his architectural practice while waiting for the bourbon to soften me up. I enjoyed those late winter evenings when the sleet lashed the leaded windows and the firelight danced on the brass andirons.

I felt somewhat less enthusiasm for the periods of compulsory athletics that followed. They were a lot of work.

The first time Jack lunged at me, I thought he was joking. After all, he had known me for years—since the days when I wore a crew cut and a mustache. We had lost touch for a while, but one day I saw him on Michigan Avenue and called out to him. He had always been loath to pass up any woman so long as she remained ambulatory, so he stopped to chat with a quizzical smile while he rummaged about inside his head to find my name. "I'm Nancy Hunt," I told him, "but I used to be. . . ." The next week he phoned me and invited me out to lunch.

So I hardly expected him to take a physical interest in me, and indeed I laughed and tried to push him away the first time he did. But I was also grateful, sexual acceptance having come to represent the highest form of recognition, and I did my best to accommodate him. Into my bed I took him— a hairy satyr with a pot belly and little tufts of hair that stuck up like horns on either side of his head—and manfully he had at me. But this was before my steel-driving man; no one had yet achieved what Jack was then attempting, and his stamina wasn't equal to his ambitions. So he gave it up as a bad job, and I had to bring him ease by other means. Then he rolled over and fell asleep, leaving my thirst unquenched. He had not kissed me or held me in his arms or told me I was beautiful. He had merely accepted my ministrations as if they were his right and then fallen asleep amid a stench of sweat and semen. I lay awake beside him, irritated and unfulfilled, as I often would again. I tried to find solace in realizing I wasn't the first woman to be left in such a state.

After my steel-driving man had blazed the trail for him, Jack did better, though not much. He held the view that his release was my job, and mine would take care of itself. Moreover, he refused to come to my apartment again after that first time but insisted that we always sleep at his place, where I had neither makeup nor clean clothes nor nightgown nor orange juice. Sometimes when we had finished, I would get up and dress and take a taxi home at three o'clock, merely for the comfort of my own bathtub and orange juice for breakfast.

It wasn't these irritations that derailed us, however, but my stubborn insistence on winning just one point. I conceded everything else: We met when he pleased and ate what he chose and slept in his bed. But I became irrationally fixed on the notion that he should take me out to eat at a restaurant. I knew he ate at restaurants almost every day of his life, and I didn't see why he couldn't take me with him just once. I didn't care whether it was for lunch or supper, whether it was French cuisine or franchise chicken. I just wanted to enjoy the symbolic act of being taken out on a date, as if we had a conventional relationship. But he steadfastly refused, no matter how I pleaded and nagged. Months later, when it was too late, I told him why I had left him, and he was surprised. Did I really mean that all I had wanted was to be taken out to eat at a restaurant? He hadn't known it was so important to me.

I met Saul at the Corona bar one night when I was having a suppertime bourbon to help me forget about Jack. He was sitting on the stool next to mine, both of us eating salted peanuts from the same glass bowl. I don't remember how we started talking, but he was soon telling me about his business and then about his flying. I felt a familiar stirring. My instinct had led me once more to a pilot. He even owned an airplane: a high-performance Rockwell Commander with retractable gear. I had always liked small airplanes and on a couple of occasions had been allowed to put my hands and feet on the controls of one and fly it briefly.

"If you ever want to go for an airplane ride, just give me a ring," Saul said, handing me his business card.

When I got back to the newsroom, I tossed the card in the wastebasket. The next week, the copy desk phone rang for me.

"How would you like to come over to the Corona for a drink and some salted peanuts?" asked a pleasant male voice that I couldn't identify.

"Sure, I'd like that," I said impulsively, and then was forced to add lamely, "Who is this?"

It was Saul.

Over the next two weeks, he paid me the most assiduous attention. For our second date, he picked me up after a doctor's appointment and took me to lunch in a Greek restaurant, then drove us to Meigs Field to watch the airplanes. He turned into the Adler Planetarium parking lot and stopped near the center and waited with his engine running. Presently a Piper Navajo came floating down directly toward us, its landing gear extended as if to push its wheels through our windshield, then cleared the car by seventy-five feet and touched down on the field behind us. I laughed and clapped my hands with delight, and Saul was grinning with self-satisfaction. He had deliberately positioned us just short of Runway 18, knowing that one of the big corporate twins would descend almost on top of us—as if at his command, for my private entertainment.

That weekend he came up to my apartment for a drink, and when I asked him if he would like another, he refused, saying he had to get home because *they* were going out for dinner that night.

"You're married?" I asked, annoyed. I don't know why I'd never thought about it before.

"Yes."

"Then what are you doing here?"

"I'm just having a drink with you," he said, grinning pleasantly.

It was impossible to be angry with him. He had made me no promises and had taken nothing from me. He had never touched me except to kiss me hello or good-bye, and that had been more my idea than his. He really was just having a drink with me, and if I wanted to make something of that innocuous pastime, then *my* mind was dirty, not his. I knew, of course, that he wouldn't be cultivating my friendship if he didn't intend to make love to me eventually, but he was far too clever and dominant to let me set the pace. Like Jack before him, he insisted on calling the tunes.

Almost every afternoon he telephoned me on the copy desk and asked me out for a drink. He wasn't a drinking man by nature, but we needed someplace to meet, so we would go to one of the crowded bars near Tribune Tower. I would order a Beck's beer and he would order a vodka and tonic, and we would give ourselves over to the pleasures of exploratory conversation. It was May, the air was warm, and we both felt young.

One Saturday I invited him on a picnic, nothing elaborate. I wore navy-blue shorts and a print halter top. He brought his transistor radio. We walked over to Lincoln Park, where we found a place on the grass amid all the gay couples who go there to sunbathe. We set up the charcoal grill, and he lit it, and when the coals were burning gray with ash, I put on the hamburgers. It was a heavenly, sunny day. We lay on the grass, sipping beer and talking.

Late in the afternoon he took me home. There in my apartment he crossed the living room to me and put his arms around me and held me silently. Just that. He wasn't overmastering me or pleading with me. He was declaring himself at last, and I could have him or not as I pleased. I turned my face up to him to be kissed.

Saul was the most skilled and considerate lover that woman was ever blessed with. And the most self-controlled. He could make love for an hour without losing command of himself or of me. I had read that the pleasures of the bed could be made to last that long and longer, but I had never believed it nor tried to do it myself. At first I thought that, like Jack, he merely had trouble reaching climax, and I tried to hasten him on, but he reined me gently and guided us at his own tempo. He lifted me to peaks that I had never dreamed existed and he laughed with pleasure at my rapture. And because men like to know when they are pleasing you, I allowed myself to moan and thrash without inhibition. I had never imagined I could feel like this—so aroused, so tender, so physically sensitive. No man had ever done this to me.

For that matter, few men have done it to me since. For me—as I suspect for most genetic women—orgasm is an elusive pleasure, often stubbornly truant when most courted, sometimes overtaking me when least expected. I have had men try all the standard techniques while I remained as cool and disinterested as a bank teller. At other times, alone, I have found myself throbbing erotically while listening to Mozart. Granted his health and a reasonable degree of sobriety, a man can almost always be stimulated to the point of ejaculation. As a woman, I have no comparable assurance. When it happens, the sensation manifests itself as a series of pulsations, much like those I once felt as a man but more diffuse and less assaultive. It is at once both of shorter duration and more prolonged, sometimes subsiding only to rise again with still greater insistence. It has never happened to me during penetration, but with Saul it often occurred during those delicious preludes of amorous play. He knew exactly how to achieve it, and I think he enjoyed my climax as much as his own.

We made love as often as he could get away from his office in the morning, which was seldom more than once or twice a week. Weekends he usually spent with his family, a loyalty I couldn't criticize, though I took some satisfaction from my belief that his wife couldn't respond to him as passionately as I could, with my first-hand knowledge of male sexual pleasure. Besides, I had church on Sunday mornings and the apartment to clean and laundry to wash. And almost every day, either in the morning when I was at home or in the afternoon at work, he would phone me for no purpose but to talk and ask if I was all right. It was enough. I was happy.

Curiously, the promised airplane ride failed to materialize. I didn't press him, supposing that he didn't want the men at the airport to see him with a woman other than his wife. Saul was methodical in keeping the different parts of his life in their proper compartments, and I respected such orderly habits, so lacking in myself. But I was growing jealous of his airplane and of the people he permitted to share his flying life while excluding me. Knowing its importance to him, I wanted to experience that part of him as well.

Failing that, I arose on Memorial Day with a newborn resolution: I didn't need him to take me flying; I could fly myself. Without a moment's hesitation, I went out, rented a car, and drove to the airport.

"Have you got any instructors who aren't doing anything right now?" I asked in the flight office. An instructor was found for me, and I went up for my first hour in a Cessna

150. Now I knew what Saul saw and felt when he flew from this same field. It was very beautiful. By the time I drove home, I had signed up for lessons for the next three weeks.

I told Saul about it the next evening over drinks at the Pioneer Court bar, somewhat diffidently because I didn't know how he would react to my taking this step into his preserve. I opened my purse and brought out my brand-new logbook. "You mean you carry it around with you?" he asked with a bemused grin. He tried not to show it, but I think he really was a little piqued. Flying was for men, and I was clearly and demonstrably a woman. "You're just like a little girl," he had told me fondly in bed one morning, adding so that I shouldn't take it amiss, "I think it's delightful."

He lectured me sternly and often now, asserting that flying was serious business and if I was going to do it, I must put my whole mind to it because anything less would get me killed (most military-trained pilots like Saul feel that way). I listened to him solemnly and resolved that I would model my attitude on his, either flying by the book or not flying at all.

At first I had an awful time. Though I knew I mustn't, I overcontrolled the airplane, chased the altimeter needle around the dial, gained and lost two hundred feet at a time, dipped first one wing and then the other. I was all over the sky. I think my instructor was scared of me, probably with good reason. One afternoon when I was practicing climbing turns, I noticed that the ball in the turn-and-slip indicator was far off center, and momentarily I forgot the proper way to correct this. At something very near stall speed and holding right aileron, I kicked in left rudder. The airplane gave a convulsive shudder of protest and started reeling crazily. The instructor seized the controls and restored us to equilibrium. "Never do that!" he stormed, white-faced. "You'll put the airplane into a spin." I had assumed that he knew how to recover from a spin, and it made me uneasy to think that he could be so easily rattled. I hadn't done it on purpose.

"How did it go today?" Saul asked me on the phone that afternoon.

I told him, embellishing the story for comic effect, but his laughter was strained. Saul had difficulty in seeing anything funny about mishandling airplanes.

Pete and I went out to supper one night, and I told him about Saul in the objective manner that many years in the newspaper business had taught me.

"You sound as if you're in love with him," Pete commented.

I denied it, though the idea had recently occurred to me. Saul and I had been in bed, and just as he reached climax, he had cried out like Christ crucified, "Ohhh! Do you love me?" It was not a declaration of love, but rather a request that I love him. I hadn't thought he wanted me to love him, but I knew that to do so would require no effort on my part and would be a small enough gift to him when he had given me so much.

It wasn't what he had bought me—aside from a few lunches and drinks, he had never given me a present in the three months I'd known him. But he had given me a sense of security, and of being cherished. He kept track of how I spent each minute of my life—what hours I worked, which mornings I had flying lessons, what days I volunteered at the hospital, what time I went to church. Periodically I would recite my schedule for him, and he would commit it to memory. He was the only one in the world who always knew where I was—or cared.

Two or three mornings a week now I was out at the airport. I had rid myself of my apprehensive instructor and was flying with one I liked. Slowly I learned how to control the airplane and even to trim it so that it flew hands-off. But my landings remained deplorable.

"Right rudder!" my instructor would shout. "Watch where you're heading! You're going to run off the runway doing that. You could damage the gear."

It was my one big problem, and I couldn't understand it. I knew how to fly the airplane well enough, but every time I landed, my directional control fell apart. Hour after hour I flew "touch-and-go's," an exhausting exercise in which you never make a full-stop landing but always apply full power as soon as you're down on the runway, turn off the carburetor heat, retract the flaps, and take off again. Two hours of this on a gusty day with turbulence and a crosswind would leave me wrung out and discouraged. I relied on Saul's telephone calls at the office to restore me.

"Hi there, Nancy-Nancy, how did it go today? Did you fly?"

I would tuck my head down over the receiver and try to insulate myself from my surroundings, shutting out the copy editor two feet to my right and the slot man who had just taken the call and who by this time must have known Saul's voice almost as well as mine.

"Oh Baby, it makes me so darned mad! I know I can fly that airplane—I really can. But I lose it every time on the roll-out. This morning I was shooting touch-and-go's on two-four right . . ."

"You must have been getting a lot of turbulence on final as you were coming in over those trees."

"It was just murder! I thought the wings were going to come off the stupid airplane. And every time . . ."

240

Sometimes we would talk flying for fifteen or twenty minutes while edition copy piled up around me and the slot man became more and more impatient. Those calls were our main contact with each other. Saul had stopped coming over on my supper hour because he found it too hard to go back to work in the evenings after drinking.

Conscientious pilots tend not to drink much, and under Saul's influence I reduced my own drinking to one or two weekend evenings when I was neither flying nor working. Smoking also inhibits a pilot's perceptions. Saul didn't smoke, so I gave it up. I even stopped drinking coffee in the office. I gained three pounds that I couldn't lose no matter how I dieted, but I wanted to stay healthy, both for flying and for him.

Once or twice a week he would call me at home. "Do you feel like having company this morning?" he would ask.

It was a good time to see him. We would both be well rested, both freshly bathed, both ardent. We would have coffee at the dining table and talk, or more usually he would talk while I listened. Sometimes he discoursed on current events, sometimes he would embroider on incidents from his own activities. He had a sensitive ear for people's words and the feelings that lay behind them, and he would reconstruct whole conversations and scenes for my amusement.

"I'd better be going or I won't get any work done today," he would say. He had no intention of going.

I would rise and kiss him good-bye, and our arms would lock around each other, and the kiss would last and last.

"I've got to go to the bathroom," I would say.

When I came back he would be in the bedroom, lying on my bed, the blanket and top sheet pulled back, his clothes folded on top of the laundry hamper. He would smile at me lovingly and get up to help me undress. He looked half his age with his glasses off. His body was lean and well muscled, his skin firm and supple. He was surprisingly strong. Sometimes when I was lying on the bed so that he could not get at me conveniently, he would put his arm under the small of my back and slide me down as easily as he adjusted the seat in his airplane. He wouldn't ask; he just did it. It made me feel terribly submissive and female. But even submissive females are permitted some initiative in bed. I reached for him.

When he had found release, he sometimes fell asleep—right there on the spot, exactly as he lay. The first time it happened we had our arms around each other, and as I looked into his sleeping face, I was swept with a tide of tenderness. Only at such moments was I permitted to see him as a fallible mortal like me.

Inevitably I grew bored with my role as pliant female and dominated partner. I yearned to exert some control over our lives. Once I provoked a quarrel in an attempt to gain some dominion—or at least a taste of equality—but Saul wouldn't allow himself to be baited. He made one overture toward peace, and when I had angrily spurned it, he left me to simmer until I grew so lonely for him that I had to call him at his office and ask him to please take me out on my supper break. I should have been warned by that experience.

By now I had had more than thirty hours of dual but had not been allowed to solo. Many student pilots solo after twelve hours; most do so by twenty. I was still grinding around the pattern doing touch-and-go's, disgusted with myself and humiliated that I couldn't do better for Saul. If he didn't value me—as a pilot as well as a woman—then I had no value in my own eyes.

"You're learning to fly?" Jack asked incredulously. I had met him by chance on Michigan Avenue one evening during my supper break.

"What's so funny about that? The fact of the matter is that I can fly very well." Yes, I could fly, but I couldn't land.

"All right, Nancy," he said good-humoredly. "I'm sure you can. Now tell me about this man you've got."

"He's very nice to me—nicer than you were—and I like him a lot. A lot."

I had liked Jack a lot too, though not as much as he had assumed. "You're in love with me," he had insisted one night with that insufferable air of the man who knows a great deal more than you do.

Saul never talked like that.

We were lying with our heads on the same pillow, spent and happy.

"Baby?" I asked softly.

"Umm?" he answered.

"There's something that's been bothering me."

"What's that, Sweetheart?"

"Well, the last two Sundays at church, the readings have mentioned fornication. I'm really not all that religious, but it is part of the Judeo-Christian ethic that it's bad to go around fornicating all the time. So nowadays people excuse it by saying that it's an expression of love or at least of affection. And I'll buy that; I think that's a valid reason. And I am fond of you, and I think you're fond of me."

"Uh-huh."

"So I was thinking that maybe if we acted more as if we were fond of each other, I wouldn't feel so much like a whore, and maybe we could go out and eat together once in a while like a normal couple." There it was again, just as it had been with Jack. Even though he was married and I worked nights, I wanted something resembling a normal dating-life.

Saul pulled me toward him and kissed my forehead. "I understand what you're saying. Sure, we can go out to eat sometimes."

And we did, but it always happened like everything else: when he said and on his initiative. I still called none of the shots.

Yet I was content with him, even with this one minor adjustment that I wanted to make in our relationship. . . .

"How would you like to stop by my place for a nightcap after work?" It was Jack on the copy-desk phone, with the same old invitation clothed in the same tattered disguise. I hadn't seen Saul for several days, and I was lonely.

"I'd like that, but I'm not going to go to bed with you."

"That's a hell of a thing to say! Do you think every man in the world wants to go to bed with you? You're assuming a whole lot there."

"Okay, I'd like to have a nightcap with you, but I just don't want you to think I'm going to go to bed with you, because I'm not."

"Why not? Are you getting religious or something?"

"No, I'm not getting religious or something, but I'm already sleeping with one guy, and I'm not clever enough to juggle two." It had nothing to do with cleverness, either. I just didn't want to sleep with anyone except Saul.

I went up to Jack's place after work, stopping on the way to buy a six-pack of beer because I knew better than to let him dope me with one of those glass mugs filled to the brim with bourbon. I needn't have feared. Jack accepted my new virtuousness with good grace. After a kiss of greeting, he sat beside me on the sofa and never laid a hand on me.

"Are you still taking flying lessons?"

"Sure."

"And how are things going with what's-his-name?"

Again I told him Saul's name. I told him how Saul could read the feelings in what people said and recreate entire scenes for me days later. I told him about the places Saul had taken me for lunch and the way he called me every afternoon.

"I'm jealous," Jack said. "I'm happy for you, but I'm jealous."

The next Saturday afternoon, I flew a cross-country to Rockford, and there at last I soloed. My instructor endorsed my student pilot certificate and climbed out onto the ramp, and for the first time I found myself alone in an airplane. I taxied to the end of the runway, called the tower for clearance, and took off. The airplane climbed a little faster without the instructor's weight, but otherwise the flight differed not at all from the scores I had made before. I had wondered if I would be frightened when the responsibility rested entirely in my hands and was relieved to find that I wasn't. A quarter of a mile beyond the end of the runway, I made my first turn above a web of high-tension lines and their supporting pylons, which reached hungrily for me. They couldn't harm me. I knew how to fly. I made three solo landings that day, none of them dangerously bad. The jinx was broken. I wished I could celebrate with Saul, but he never saw me on Saturdays now.

Two days later, I flew with the head of the flight school, who discovered that, despite my long legs, when seated in the airplane I had trouble seeing over the instrument panel. He told me to sit on a cushion, and now my landings really improved. If I could see the runway when I was landing, I could keep the airplane on it. I was sorry I had had to pay for thirty hours of dual to learn this, but I was glad to have found it out at last. It worked like a charm when I flew again two days later.

"Hi there, Daughter, how did it go today? Did you fly?" It was Saul on the copy-desk phone.

"Hi, Baby. Sure, and I soloed again too. We went down to Joliet."

"You must have had a terrific crosswind on that runway three-zero down there. It's been right out of the west here all day."

"Oh, you'd have been so proud of me, Baby! We did have an awful crosswind—fifteen knots gusting to twenty, smack on the left side, and I just did everything right: left wing down and right rudder to hold the nose straight. You should have heard my instructor. He was shouting, 'You're too high! You're too high!' but I didn't pay any attention to him. I just shut him out because I knew what I was going to do. I wanted plenty of airspeed to get me through the turbulence, and then when I was almost over the fence, I chopped the power and popped full flaps and put it down on one wheel. Oh Baby, it was just a classic landing, a textbook example! After that I shot three landings by myself."

"Hey, that's great, Sweetie!"

I was feeling terribly pleased with myself, and I suggested he come over and buy me a drink on my supper break to celebrate and to help me take my mind off a vile toothache. But he said he had too much work to do.

The next day—a Thursday—my tooth was bothering me a lot. I wished that I could tell Saul about it, but he had flown the Commander to Michigan on an overnight business trip, so I wouldn't even have the solace of his afternoon telephone call. I'd gotten up at 2:00 A.M. and taken some Valium to ease the pain, but it hadn't helped. Friday morning I went to see my dentist, and was told the tooth would have to go. An eddy of grief spun me as the tooth was pried out, though I could not feel it physically. I was racked by emotional trauma—by a sense of loss and an awareness of advancing age. My teeth were coming out! Oh my Baby, I need you now.

By then I wasn't even certain that he was alive. That morning, when he was due to fly home from Michigan, a series of thunderstorms had rolled across the city with heavy rains and high, gusty winds—the sort of storm that can easily destroy a light airplane. He was a superb pilot, but sometimes even the best can be caught by a faulty weather forecast.

He called at last, shortly after I had started work. "Hi there, Nancy-Nancy. How has your day been?"

"I've had a terrible day. They pulled my tooth out. Baby, I'm so glad you're all right! We had the most awful thunderstorms here all morning, and I didn't know when you were flying home, and I was so worried about you."

He told me about his flight with specific attention to winds aloft, indicated airspeed, computed ground speed, and type of flight plan filed.

I told him about my tooth and how miserable I felt. "Baby, can you please come over? I need you."

"Not today, I'm afraid. I've got a lot of work to catch up on here, and I want to get away early this evening. I'm going to go up to Wisconsin fishing this weekend."

"Baby!" I cried out. I hadn't seen him for seven whole days, and I was not to see him for two days more.

The slot man was gesturing at me urgently. One of the stories for which I was responsible needed extensive revision in the Midwest Replate edition, and the deadline was galloping down on us.

"I'll give you a ring Monday morning after I get back," Saul was saying.

"Come on, Nancy!" the slot man barked.

The tears were welling up in my eyes, though I knew better than to let Saul hear me crying. He didn't like scenes.

"But Baby, I haven't even seen you since I soloed!" I protested. The words came out as a rasping whisper, so taut was my self-control.

"What did you say, Daughter? I can't hear you."

The sobs were rising inside me, exerting an intolerable pressure against the back of my throat. I couldn't hold them in much longer.

"Nothing. Have a nice weekend, Baby. Good-bye."

Then, for the first time in my newspaper career, I cried on the copy desk.

I went out after work that night with two other women copy editors and drank a great deal. Leaving them, I went to the neighborhood bar where I had met my steel-driving man and found someone to buy me another drink that I didn't need. He was the kind of man that Saul would have detested: a bearded, leather-jacketed motorcyclist, and unemployed. For that matter, Saul would have been appalled to see me drunk. Despite his lusty appetite in bed, he was something of a puritan. ("Put your robe on," he told me once severely after we had made love. "You don't like me to go wandering around in front of you bare-arsed naked?" I asked teasingly. "No, I don't," he snapped.)

"You've got a lot of class," the bearded motorcyclist was telling me. Oh God! "You live around here?"

"Right around the corner," I said perversely.

"Why don't we go up to your place?"

"Because I'd rather sleep alone." I gathered up my purse

and the last of my scattered wits and lurched out the door.

Saul called me Monday morning as he had promised. "Do you feel like having some company this morning?" he asked cheerfully.

"Not very much," I lied. I was aching for him so much that I hurt, but it was the only answer left to me if I wanted to preserve some tiny bit of dignity or to prove that I was my own person, that I gave myself to this man by choice and not because I was an object of no value that anyone could have for the taking.

"How about lunch, then?"

"No, I don't think so."

"Sandwich?"

"No."

"Are you feeling all right? You sound sick."

"I feel rotten. Look, Baby, you went away and left me alone for nine whole days. I needed you, I needed you a lot, and you wouldn't come to me. I can't let you do that to me again. I love you, and it hurts too much."

"Hooo boy!" he sighed. "What a mess!"

"Why? Because I love you? What's so terrible about that? You knew I loved you." I'd finally told him one day in bed.

"Wow! That way lies madness!"

He had arranged everything so neatly in little compartments: his airplane, his business, his family, his mistress. And now I was trying to upset his system. Madness!

"I may not see you anymore," I said, feeling reckless now, "but you can't stop me from loving you. I don't need your permission for that."

"We'll have to figure out what we're going to do," he said. "I'll call you at the end of the week."

But he didn't call.

I ran into him again that Thursday during my supper break. I was in the Corona bar, where we had first met and he had offered me an airplane ride. I was drinking bourbon and eating salted peanuts and wishing I were dead. And I was smoking again.

Saul walked in behind another woman, and I gave him only a slight wave of recognition because I didn't want to upset his arrangements, though my heart felt shriveled. But the woman wasn't with him; he was alone. He came and stood beside me and at last sat down and began telling me about his airplane.

"What are you talking about?"

"I'm just trying to make conversation," he said reproachfully. ("I'm just having a drink with you," he had said ages ago.)

"Did you know that we haven't seen each other for thirteen days?"

"No, I didn't know that."

"Are you glad to see me? Am I pretty?"

"You look very nice."

We were saying all the wrong things. I had to go back to work.

I didn't see Saul again for several months, and then we met as friends, no longer lovers. But after a prolonged failure of nerve, I resumed my flying lessons. That September I spent a two-week vacation at a Florida flight school and earned my private pilot's certificate. At least I had that much to mark Saul's passage.

FIFTEEN

There's nothing like a sex change to make you realize how tightly you are wedged into the bureaucrats' filing cabinets. From the moment the obstetrician makes out your birth certificate, they have you tagged, and the older you get, the more firmly they staple you into your assigned manila folder: baptismal certificate, high school record, college transcript, Social Security file, driver's license, credit cards, income tax returns . . . until you are pinned immovably like a butterfly in a glass case with a classification card affixed beneath. If you try to wriggle off your pin, the curators rush to prevent you, not because they bear you any ill will, but because they object to the disruption of their system.

Yet it is possible to arrange a transfer to a different pin with a revised classification card. As sex-reassignment surgery has grown more common—though not yet commonplace—the bureaucrats have been forced to set up procedures for altering records. Almost every state now permits a change of name and sex designation on birth certificates and driver's licenses, though in no way have they made the process easy. To change my own birth certificate, the New York City department of health demanded five separate documents:

· Court order granting a name change.

· Detailed report of examination prior to operation; surgical record, including date of operation and postoperative examination, signed by the surgeon. [I had a tough time with this one because Futrell obstinately refused to let me have a copy of the surgical record and New York refused to change my birth certificate without it.]

· Postpsychiatric evaluation signed by the attending psychiatrist. [I never saw a psychiatrist after the surgery, so I asked a friend to write this one. He wrote in part, "Ms. Hunt is a woman at peace with herself. . . ." He said it was a love letter.]

· New certificate of birth signed by the psychiatrist or surgeon. [Futrell signed this, which means that he presided at my birth some ten years before his own.]

· Certified, paid copy of the old birth certificate, or a three-dollar fee to pay for one.

The first requirement, in turn, forced me to go to court to get a legal name-change. I hadn't planned to do that. By law, you can call yourself anything you please as long as you don't do it to defraud someone, so I had merely started to call myself "Nancy" and let the legality of it go. But it's not hard to do the thing officially in Chicago. The standard lawyer's fee for the job is two hundred dollars, but you can do it yourself and save money. The process involves filling out a sheaf of petition forms, paying thirty-four dollars to publish the change in the *Chicago Law Bulletin,* and appearing in court six weeks later with another thirty-two dollars to cover the cost of filing.

It seemed like a lot of trouble just to change my name on my birth certificate, a document I hadn't had to produce for years. I would need it if I were going to apply for a passport, but I already had a passport.

Until recently, the United States tourist passport didn't state the bearer's sex, which was a lucky omission for trans-sexuals and transvestites. Of course, it did give the bearer's first name, and if he happened to be named John or Thomas, he had a problem. My former name, however, was sexually ambiguous. When Ellen and I went to Europe in the summer of 1975, my old passport having expired, I acquired a new one by presenting a photograph of myself in long hair, print blouse, and a winning smile. I crossed half a dozen borders without a hitch. (Ellen, curiously enough, ran into difficulty with customs at Heathrow airport in London and had to submit to a special interrogation while I stood by looking decorative.) The new passports do state the bearer's sex, but I had that filled in properly when I had them change my name.

The State of Illinois will change the sex designation on a driver's license upon presentation of three dollars and a letter from the surgeon attesting that he has altered the anatomy.

"Is this the right place to get a change made in my driver's license?"

"What kind of change?"

"Sex change."

"This is the right place." They were all helpful and terribly interested.

My bank didn't care what I called myself so long as I didn't bounce any checks. When Ellen threatened to take me to the cleaners, I closed our joint accounts and opened new ones in my new name with new checks. It couldn't have been easier.

Most surprising of all was the ease with which I changed my name on the records of the *Chicago Tribune,* though I wouldn't have been surprised if I'd thought about it. Women employees change their names all the time when they marry, and the *Tribune* has printed forms to assist them. Just put your old name on the line where it says "Maiden Name" and your new name on the next line, and they take care of everything: payroll department, house telephone directory, personnel file, withholding tax, Social Security. I agonized over that step for six months and performed it in three minutes.

Credit cards were an altogether more difficult and unpleasant matter. The world of commerce is prepared to accept the fact that women change their last names when they get married or divorced, but it takes a dim view of people who change their first names. The law prohibits denial of credit on the basis of sex, but that doesn't prevent creditors from imputing fraudulent intent when a customer whom they have always regarded as a man asks that the name on the account be changed to "Nancy." And they have sufficient reason for suspicion. It's not uncommon for newly divorced women to try to substitute their own names for their ex-husbands' as they try to gain control of charge accounts.

That's what BankAmericard thought I was up to when I

asked to change the name on my account. No matter that I wrote them long letters assuring them that I was the same person with the same Social Security number, the same employment and credit history, the same blood type and morals and political affiliations. They smelled a rat, and they were damned if they were going to let me con them into surrendering my ex-husband's account to me. They could have settled the issue with a two-minute phone call to the *Tribune*; a newspaper reporter would have done that by reflex. After six months, they phoned me one afternoon. We debated the question unprofitably for ten minutes until I saw that I was going to lose and reluctantly divulged my circumstances. "You are quite right, I used to be a man," I confessed wearily. "I have had sex-change surgery and am now a woman, and I want a new credit card to reflect that fact. Is that what you wanted to know?"

The credit investigator was horrified at having blundered into this awful revelation. "That's all right then, ma'am," he said in a shaken voice.

"You mean I can have my new card now?"

"Yes, ma'am. There won't be any more trouble, ma'am."

And there wasn't. I got my new BankAmericard within a week.

I had a similar experience with Marshall Field's, but this time I tried to be forearmed. I went down to their credit office in person, bringing with me a handful of photo I.D.s with both my old and new names so that there should be no doubt that I was the same person. But the woman I talked to was so trusting that she never asked to see all this documentation. "You'll have your new card in two weeks," she promised.

But the new card did not arrive, and so I presented myself

again at Marshall Field's credit office. This time I was received with suspicion and even hostility. My request would not be granted, I was told. I asked if I could please talk to a supervisor. Yes, if I would wait a good, long time. I waited.

The supervisor who at last appeared was a stoop-shouldered hangdog with mistrustful eyes. His nasty instincts had led him to conclude, not that I was my own ex-husband, as BankAmericard had thought, but that I was my own brother. Nor could I shake his belief in this peculiar notion.

Despairing of any successful appeal through reason, I decided to try him out on picture recognition. I threw down on the desk before him my old *Tribune* I.D. with my old name and my new I.D. that designated me as "Nancy." He stiffened for a moment as if he had felt an electric shock.

I had intended next to dazzle him with my Chicago police department press pass, which identified me by my old name but clearly showed me to be a woman, but I was trembling with rage. I no longer wanted to convince him; I wanted to annihilate him. Reaching into my purse, I flung down before him a letter signed by Futrell. "To Whom It May Concern: This is to confirm that [my old name] has a diagnosis of male transsexualism and has undergone gender-reassignment surgery such that at present her anatomic sex matches that of her female psychological gender."

He read it in a state of confusion.

"Well," he said, forcing a sickly smile, "this is all we needed to know."

"You didn't need to know it," I answered, suddenly feeling very tired and fearing that I might cry. "It's none of your business."

He had them make out a new card for me while I waited.

The matter of changing one's name assumes an importance to the transsexual that transcends the needs of business. Given a man's name, the necessity is obvious, but I was under no such compulsion since my old name could serve for either man or woman. But just let a transsexual out of the hospital with her sex-change certificate in her hand, and ninety-nine times out of a hundred she'll head straight for a lawyer's office to get all her papers put in her new name. I know of one lawyer in Chicago who specializes in this work.

Invariably the name chosen will be unmistakably feminine, Cynthia, Suzanne, Diana, and Anne being among those of my acquaintance. Sometimes they are superfeminine—Gigi, Fifi, Darlene, and the like.

I chose my own name with Ellen's help one evening long before I knew that I would in fact become a woman and carry that name for the rest of my life. I had thought I was a weekend transvestite. I started through the list of "Common English names" in the back of my *Webster's Collegiate Dictionary:* Abigail, Ada, Adaline, Adela, Adelaide—none of them appealed to me. Camilla, Candace, Carlotta, Carmel—no, no, no. Dagmar, Daphne, Deborah, Delia—none of those.

"Elizabeth. How about Elizabeth?" I asked hopefully. I had always liked that one.

"No, that's a yukky name," Ellen said. She was beginning to lose interest in the game.

I plowed through the list until I came to "Nancy," and on this I laid special stress. Ellen gave her approval—more to shut me up, I suspect, than out of any fondness for the name. And so I became Nancy, to my joy. It had been my favorite name since the fourth grade, when I read an English children's book in which one of the main characters was named Nancy. It had the added merit of embodying a concealed joke: The Random House dictionary defines a *nance* first as "an effeminate male" and second as "a male homosexual, esp. one who assumes the female role." Though I wasn't a homosexual, I was certainly assuming the female role. I doubt that anyone else ever saw the joke, and I never explained it to Ellen, but I always enjoyed it. It seemed to make the name more appropriate.

Perhaps the psychological importance of the new name is that it serves as a constant reminder and symbol of hard-won womanhood. It always pleases me to hear myself called "Nancy," just as it delights me to be called "ma'am," "young lady," "hon," "dear," "darling," "baby," and all the other names that women are subject to.

"Can I make you a sandwich before you go?" I asked the Marshall Field's man who had just finished installing a new slipcover. It was lunchtime.

"No thanks, Hon. I've got to run."

I didn't consider it an impertinence. I was pleased.

Conversely, when anyone forgot that I was henceforth to be called "Nancy" and referred to with the feminine pronoun, I was hurt and angry. I took it as a denial of my sex, which I had had to fight for while theirs had been handed to them free.

This compulsion to adopt a woman's name along with a woman's gender springs from the same root as all the other transsexual cravings—for beauty and grace, for pretty clothes, for the attention of men. Such longings don't arise from a base of reason, though I can construct a reasonable argument that it is preferable to be a woman (and for a fee could argue just as cogently for the superiority of being a man).

Moreover, I would be hard put to find any universal

agreement on what it means to be either woman or man. To me, a woman is gentle, comforting, sensitive, and above all giving. She nurtures—in the kitchen, in bed, in the sickroom —submerging her own needs to the more urgent demands of men. In contrast, men are strong, brave, protective, and good at opening recalcitrant jar tops. Certainly these conventional attributes cannot stand the test of reason, and I know a dozen women who would challenge them furiously. Women's liberationists will quickly point out that they display strength, bravery, and an ability to unscrew jar tops quite equal to any man's, and they are right. They can also point out—though they seldom do—that men often display gentleness, sensitivity, and generosity to equal any woman's. They will certainly disapprove of my eagerness to embrace the womanly stereotypes at a time when progressive feminism is denying them. I have been laughed at for my unwillingness to hook up my own stereo, taken to task for my pleasure in embroidery, and excluded from dinner parties for my enjoyment of male strength.

I cannot explain my attitudes, let alone defend them. Male transsexuals habitually say that they "feel like a woman," but no biological male—and probably no woman either—can state categorically how it feels to be a woman; someone would inevitably point out a thousand exceptions to any proposed rule. Least of all can I, after half a lifetime as a man, proclaim beyond the possibility of challenge that I know what it means to "feel like a woman." How could I? I have been hardened in a boys' prep school, trained as an infantry rifleman, educated at a men's university, married and a father, and celebrated as a war correspondent. The circumstances of life have required me to be strong, brave, and protective when I would have preferred to be weak, cowardly, and sheltered. And these facts have accreted like barnacles on a sea rock, amassing a burden of maleness that I must forever drag with me. Now would I wish to shed it all. Despite my improbable transformation, I still take a perverse pride in having survived for more than forty years as a man, much as a paraplegic might boast of learning to ride a unicycle—not that I did it well but that I did it at all.

I concede, therefore, that I tread on shaky ground when I speculate about what it means to be a woman. Yet I haven't a doubt in the world that I am one and always was. Sometimes I have a chance to test this belief, as I did on a recent visit to Charlottesville. Jennifer and her roommate, Patty McClary, had given a dinner party for me and half a dozen nurses and nursing students who had taken care of me. My English scholar was there, keeping my glass filled as the talk ranged over a wide landscape. It was a lovely evening. Later, when the other guests had gone, Jennifer, Patty, and I basked in the afterglow of good wine and lasagne, and we talked about womanhood. A few weeks later, Jennifer wrote me:

"Patty and I decided you should write a treatise on femininity. You describe so perfectly, so genuinely what it means to be a woman. You make us feel good about our womanhood—so true, to hear you define what it means to you."

I feel good about my womanhood too, perhaps in part because I have paid such a terrible price for it. I have undergone four major operations and endured seven weeks in the hospital. I have suffered months of pain and infection and disgusting drainage. I have alienated my family and my oldest friends. I have lost Ellen, the best and dearest companion in all the world.

And all of this I have willingly borne, not out of any en

joyment of agony but out of acceptance, just as the diabetic accepts the amputation of a gangrenous leg: It's preferable to death.

Not that my affliction would have killed me or that I would have killed myself because of it. Many transsexuals do commit suicide, but many do not. Indeed, I suspect that many men live their whole lives in writhing unease with never a hint that their misery stems from disordered gender.

Even I, riddled though I was with the classic symptoms, did not begin a serious study of transsexualism until I was forty-five, did not become profoundly convinced that I was myself a transsexual until I was forty-seven, and did not submit to the scalpel until I was forty-nine. And had that merciful knife been denied me, undoubtedly I would have continued to stumble along as a man.

Then why bother? Why run the risk of arrest and disgrace by dressing up in drag and venturing upon the public streets in an incongruous wig and a face slathered with pancake? Why devote an hour a week for four years to the eradication of a beard, flinching as each individual whisker is pulled out by the roots? Why spend $1,100 on hair transplants? Why wrench one's body chemistry and assume the risk of breast cancer by ingesting estrogens? Why sacrifice the organs so cherished by the members of one's own genetic sex?

"Couldn't he just be a feminine man?" asked Ellen's mother when told the worst about me.

No, I could not.

Half a dozen less drastic alternatives were available to me. If I wanted to wear floral shirts and long hair, heaven knows they had come into vogue for men, along with bracelets, necklaces, perfume, nail polish, and blow-dryers. But I thought these fashions vulgar in a man.

If I wanted the love and admiration of men, I could have become a homosexual. But I had no sympathy for homosexuals and felt a positive revulsion for the coupling of two male bodies. Though I later slept with men, I remained a devout heterosexual.

If I wanted to wear skirts and lipstick, I could have been a weekend transvestite and primped and flounced about in my spare time. I tried that and derived some relief from it for two years, but inevitably I came to perceive it as playacting. I didn't want to pretend; I wanted to be.

And there lay the heart of my dilemma: I could no longer endure pretending to be something I was not. Deceit is a tiring occupation, and despite all biological evidence to the contrary, despite my military record and my Yale degree, despite my swearing and my mustache, I knew my masculinity was fraudulent. If I were ever to make peace with myself, I would have to confront not the hairy, balding, tweed-clad façade that I presented to the world, but the person who lived inside—myself, Nancy, a woman.

Perhaps the people who know my past consider my present self a fraud: a female impersonator, a synthetic product of the pharmaceutical industry and the operating room. Admittedly, I am at best only a crude facsimile of a biological woman, with neither ovaries nor uterus, dependent on hormone pills for the rest of my life, forever carrying the male Y chromosome in every cell. An impostor? Certainly by conventional standards. And my old friends can never quite forget it, never quite banish that last self-conscious qualm as they hold the door for me or kiss me good-night. "You're a good-looking woman for your age," said one to me the other night, and undoubtedly added to himself, "considering that you're really a guy."

"You're a nicer person than I am," said Jack, minutes before setting out to seduce me.

"I'm not nicer," I said. "I'm different from you."

Women do differ from men, quite apart from anatomy. And I always sensed which one I was—again quite apart from anatomy. I was not a man. I was a woman. And if my anatomy did not confirm this classification, then in the final event it was going to be easier to change my anatomy than to change myself.

I'm well enough pleased with the anatomical changes, though I could have wished for more. I would have liked to be a teen-age sex bomb with a plump fanny sheathed in a tight little skirt. I would have liked to be five inches shorter so that I could have looked up into a man's face with enormous, adoring eyes instead of gazing at him on his own level or, worse still, looking down on him. I would have liked to have larger breasts, and I could acquire some, too, if I weren't heartily tired of allowing the surgeons to go at me with scissors and knife. I would have liked to have long, silky hair and a nineteen-inch waist and small hands and feet. I would have liked to be beautiful.

But I'm content with what I got—from God, from Ellen, and from the surgeons. Even on my worst days—tired, lonely, sick, scared—I look at myself in the mirror, and I am happy. I now see in that reflection a mirror image of the person that I have always been, no longer distorted by the flickering candle-heat of society or the crazy lens of masculinity. For better or for worse, at last I am me, a woman, an honest person. By right of suffering and endurance and the Circuit Court of Cook County, I am Nancy.

Mirror Image

Nancy Hunt

He was born to a family listed in the Social Register, attended a staid New England preparatory school, graduated from Yale University, was a late World War II draftee who rose to the rank of sergeant; after the war he became a prizewinning journalist with the *Chicago Tribune* and was noted for some of the paper's finest feature writing and war correspondence; he married and fathered three children. Then, in his late forties, he became a woman.

Nancy Hunt's *Mirror Image* begins where Jan Morris's *Conundrum* left off. It is undoubtedly the most honest and acutely revealing account we have yet had of the transsexual experience. Today many thousands of men and women are living under the painful conviction that their psychological sex is the opposite of their genetic sex. Nancy Hunt tells what that is like—the multiple agonies and pressures of behaving like a man while